BREXIT-
100 DAYS OF HELL

By
Kevin Hughes

No part of this work may be copied, reprinted
or redistributed in any format,
electronically or otherwise,
without the advance permission of
the author.

Cover image of 10 Downing Street by robertsharp @ Flickr

To contact the author please email:
kevhxxx@aol.com

BREXIT – 100 DAYS OF HELL

Foreword

The result of the 2016 referendum sent shockwaves around the world and, in the intervening forty months, the aftermath has dominated the UK political agenda. With Brexit already having cost two UK Prime Ministers their jobs, and a third deadline for exiting the EU set for just 100 days away, it falls to Boris Johnson to take over the reins. Relayed predominantly through the words of those at the heart of the crisis, what follows is a non-partisan account of a summer of twists and turns, ups and downs and claims and counterclaims, all of which ensure that the issue of Brexit continues to consume the British political scene like nothing ever before.

Tuesday 23rd July 2019

100 days to Brexit

After over six weeks of campaigning and hustings, the votes are in and counted. The original cast of ten candidates have been whittled down, in a series of ballots amongst Tory MPs, to the final two contenders on whom approximately 140,000 Conservative Party members have cast their verdict. At 11.00am at the Queen Elizabeth II centre in London, the result is announced.

Boris Johnson, former Mayor of London and Foreign Secretary, has defeated his opponent, the current Foreign Secretary Jeremy Hunt, by a margin of 2 to 1 and is dutifully declared the new leader of the Conservative Party and the next Prime Minister of the United Kingdom. In his victory speech, Boris declares that 'we are going to get Brexit done on 31st October and take advantage of all the opportunities it will bring', promising to 'deliver Brexit, unite the country and defeat Jeremy Corbyn'.

Reaction to his victory is swift, with Donald Trump, The President of the USA, declaring 'a really good man is going to be the Prime Minister of the UK now' and Theresa May, the outgoing Prime Minister, promising him her 'full support from the backbenches'. The response from other quarters is less effuse, with Nicola Sturgeon, Scotland's First Minister, expressing 'profound concerns' about the prospect of Johnson leading the country, adding that she will work with other parties to 'stop Brexit and block a no deal Brexit'. Jeremy Corbyn, the Leader of the Opposition, promises to table a motion of no confidence in the new Prime Minister 'when appropriate to do so' and Jo Swinson, newly elected Leader of the Liberal Democratic Party, declares that 'Britain deserves better than Boris Johnson'.

Wednesday 24th July 2019

99 days to Brexit

After chairing her final Cabinet meeting, Theresa May heads to the House of Commons for her last session of Prime Minister's Questions. A typically terse exchange ensues between her and Jeremy Corbyn, the outgoing Prime Minister concluding their encounter with the parting shot, 'as a party leader who has accepted when her time was up, perhaps the time is now for him to do the same.'

After returning to Downing Street, Mrs May makes a short speech on the steps, accompanied by her husband Phillip, before heading off to Buckingham Palace to formally resign as Prime Minister. A short time after she has left the Palace, Boris Johnson arrives and is invited by the Queen to form a Government. In his inaugural speech as Prime Minister, outside 10 Downing Street, Johnson promises to 'restore trust in our democracy', declaring 'never mind the backstop, the buck stops here' and repeating his campaign pledge to 'come out of the EU on October 31st, no ifs or buts.'

Once inside, the new Prime Minister begins what will turn out to be the most extensive Cabinet reshuffle in over fifty years, with seventeen former Ministers either resigning or being sacked. His leadership rival, Jeremy Hunt, allegedly refuses a demotion to Defence Secretary and thus consigns himself to the backbenches, being replaced as Foreign Secretary by Dominic Raab. Johnson loyalist Priti Patel returns to Government as Home Secretary whilst the former incumbent, Sajid Javid, is promoted to Chancellor of the Exchequer. Michael Gove, another of Boris's leadership rivals, is given the role of Chancellor of the Duchy of Lancaster with responsibility for co-ordinating no deal Brexit planning.

In between the Government positions, Johnson announces the appointment of Dominic Cummings as his senior Downing Street advisor. Considered by many to have been the mastermind behind the Vote Leave campaign three years earlier, Cummings is renowned for being brusque and abrasive, having previously described the Government's Brexit strategy as 'a train wreck'.

Boris Johnson uses his first appearance in the House of Commons as Prime Minister to deliver an ultimatum to Brussels. In a question and answer session that lasts almost two and a half hours, Johnson declares that 'if an agreement is to be reached it must be clearly understood that the way to the deal goes by way of the abolition of the backstop', adding that he had already given orders that the preparation for a no deal Brexit be accelerated. In a further display of his determination to leave the EU by the 31st October, the Prime Minister announces that he will refuse to nominate a British Commissioner to join EU president-elect Ursula von der Leyen's team on 1st November.

Johnson's words are not greeted with enthusiasm at the EU, The European Commission President, Jean-Claude Juncker, stating that the remaining EU 27 countries will not give in to his demand to renegotiate the withdrawal agreement. His words are echoed by Michel Barnier, the EU's chief negotiator, who calls the Prime Minister's stance 'combative' and declares the demand for the removal of the backstop 'unacceptable'. Irish Taoiseach, Leo Varadkar, weighs in too, warning that the UK will not get a future trade deal with the EU without the backstop in place.

On the domestic front, Liberal Democrat leader Jo Swinson urges Labour to table a no-confidence motion in the new Prime Minister, accusing Jeremy Corbyn of 'aiding and abetting' the Conservatives by failing to challenge the new Government. Jeremy Corbyn responds by saying that he would 'surprise' Johnson with a motion of no confidence 'at the time of our choosing'.

On the day that the House of Commons rises for its summer recess, the tough rhetoric continues with the Prime Minister's spokesman reiterating that there would be no new talks with the European Union until they renege on their refusal to renegotiate the withdrawal agreement. 'It has been rejected three times by the House of Commons', he declares, 'it's not going to pass'. The same message is repeated by Boris Johnson during telephone calls with President Macron, Jean-Claude Juncker and Angela Merkel.

Speaking in Northern Ireland, Irish Foreign Minister, Simon Coveney, says that the new Prime Minister's comments in the House of Commons yesterday were 'very unhelpful'. He goes on to add that Johnson 'seems to have made a deliberate decision to set Britain on a collision course with the European Union and with Ireland in relation to the Brexit negotiations, and I think only he can answer the question as to why he is doing that'.

Back home, Tory MP Mark Francois, a member of the Eurosceptic parliamentary group the ERG, claims that its members would vote against any attempt to reintroduce the withdrawal agreement negotiated by Theresa May, saying that it is 'dead'. Mr Francois goes on to claim that the EU would 'blink' first and agree to talks on a free trade deal. His words are echoed by Steve Baker, a strongly Eurosceptic MP who declined an invitation to be a part of Boris's Government team. 'I fear being asked to vote for a compromise withdrawal agreement with a time limit on the backstop', Baker says, adding, 'any attempt to revive it in any form would be a complete betrayal'.

During a visit to a police training centre in Birmingham, Boris Johnson rules out calling a General Election before Britain has left the European Union. 'The British people voted in 2015, in 2016, in 2017', he says. 'What they want us to do is deliver on their mandate, come out of the EU on October 31st. They don't want another electoral event, they don't want a referendum, they don't want a General Election. They want us to deliver.'

Donald Trump, after a phone call with Boris Johnson, says that talks about a 'very substantial' trade deal with the UK are under way. A bilateral deal, the US President adds, could lead to a 'three to four, five times' increase in current trade and that negotiations would begin 'as soon as possible' after the UK leaves the EU.

Members of Parliament may be heading off on their summer holidays, but Boris Johnson continues to tour the provinces. Speaking at Manchester's Science and Industry Museum, the Prime Minister promises a faster rail link between Leeds and Manchester, claiming that the benefits would be 'colossal'. He goes on to say that full details of the trans-Pennine link would be published in the autumn, after a review of HS2, but reassures his one hundred strong audience that the proposal will 'turbo-charge the economy'.

In his first press interview as Leader of the House of Commons, Jacob Rees-Mogg states that the only way to stop Brexit is to revoke Article 50, but claims that there is not the support in the chamber to do that. Attacking those colleagues who keep 'wittering on about no deal', Rees-Mogg says that the requirement that the backstop be removed has been rebuffed by the EU and, if that remains the case, 'we leave without a deal, we keep £39 billion and the Sun will still rise on Nov 1st.'

Elsewhere in the press, Attorney General Geoffrey Cox tells 'The Times' that a no deal Brexit could happen even if MPs vote to block it and bring down the government, and could even occur partway through a snap election campaign. 'No important policy decisions should be taken which could fetter the freedom of an incoming government', he says, adding, 'no greater fetter could exist than if we irrevocably withdraw from a major treaty'.

Michael Gove, the Minister charged with preparing for Brexit, warns today that there is 'now a very real prospect' of no deal, and that the government was working on the assumption that a new agreement with Brussels would not be obtained. Writing in 'The Sunday Times' he goes on to say that mere tweaks to the thrice defeated withdrawal agreement negotiated by Theresa May would not be enough. 'You can't just reheat the dish that's been sent back and expect that will make it more palatable', he writes, adding that he hoped EU leaders might yet open up to the idea of striking a new deal, 'but we must operate on the assumption that they will not. While we are optimistic about the future, we are realistic about the need to plan for every eventuality'.

Reinforcing the contents of Gove's column, it is revealed today that Boris Johnson has set up a 'war cabinet' to deliver Brexit, by any means necessary, by 31st October. Known as XO, the committee will, according to Michael Gove, 'agree actions, make decisions and solve problems, and all with specific deadlines'. The group will consist of six members; The Prime Minister, Gove, Chancellor Sajid Javid, Foreign Secretary Dominic Raab, Brexit Secretary Steve Barclay and the Attorney General Geoffrey Cox. In addition, the Prime Minister has instructed Gove to chair meetings of civil servants and political advisers every day, including Sundays, until the referendum result is delivered.

An information blitz is to be launched by the Government to prepare Britain for a no deal Brexit. Television adverts and leaflets are to be produced to ensure every family and business is geared up to leave the EU on October 31st. The campaign, which will reputedly cost up to £10million, is likely to include sending a leaflet to 27million households setting out the facts and realities of leaving the EU without a deal.

In his first major interview since becoming Chancellor of the Exchequer, Sajid Javid tells 'The Sunday Telegraph' that he is planning a major spending blitz in preparation for a no deal Brexit, pledging 'significant extra funding' to get the country 'fully ready to leave'. He adds that 'all necessary funding will be made available' for 500 new Border Force officers and any new infrastructure that is required around Britain's ports.

The 'Mail on Sunday' today carries a claim that Dominic Cummings, Boris Johnson's senior Downing Street advisor, is planning to turn the Conservative Party conference at the end of September into a Brexit rally. The annual gathering, to be held this year in Manchester, is due to finish just 29 days before Brexit and Cummings is said to have declared that the event will be used solely to 'hammer home the Government's message that we are leaving on October 31st with or without a deal'.

Jeremy Corbyn says that the Labour Party will campaign for the UK to remain in the EU if Boris Johnson tries to implement a no deal Brexit. Speaking to Sky News, he says that he would back a second referendum which would put the Brexit deal against no deal. 'No deal we'll oppose and we think people should have a final choice on it. They can have a vote then between Remain and whatever option Boris Johnson decides to put to them at that time. If we are in power, yes of course, the same thing would apply because I want to make sure we get to the end of this process where we have a fixed position in this country. What we said is in the event of a no deal Brexit we will campaign to remain'.

Ahead of his first visit to Scotland as Prime Minister tomorrow, Ruth Davidson, the Scottish Conservative leader, warns Boris Johnson that she will not support a no deal Brexit. 'I don't think the Government should pursue a no deal Brexit and, if it comes to it, I won't support it', she says, adding, 'I wrote to tell the former Prime Minister Theresa May that last year and I confirmed my position to her successor when I spoke to him last week'.

French EU minister Nathalie Loiseau, a close ally of President Macron, warns that there would be no discussion on a future trade relationship between Britain and the EU until the divorce bill, citizen's rights and the Irish border issues are resolved. She goes on to say that Boris Johnson's threat of no deal would solve nothing and that the EU would only grant an extension to Article 50 'if there is something serious happening' like a General Election or a people's vote.

A report by The Confederation of British Industry warns that neither the UK nor the EU is ready for a no deal Brexit on 31st October. 'While the UK's preparations to date are welcome, the unprecedented nature of Brexit means some aspects cannot be mitigated', the report states, going on to add that 'although businesses have already spent billions on contingency planning for no deal, they remain hampered by unclear advice, timelines, cost and complexity'.

Foreign Secretary Dominic Raab, speaking on Radio Four, says that, while there are no 'firm plans' yet, the Government will be using the summer recess to approach 'growth markets' in Asia, Latin America and the US to push for future trade deals. He tempers his comments by going on to say that 'negotiation with the EU is crucially important and we would love to get a deal that is acceptable to the UK, but Brussels is not the only game in town'.

Boris Johnson goes to Scotland and tells journalists in Faslane, Britain's nuclear submarine base on the Clyde, that 'the Withdrawal Agreement is dead, it's got to go. But there is scope to do a new deal'. Announcing £300 million of funding for communities in Scotland, Wales and Northern Ireland, the Prime Minister goes on to call for a renewal of 'the ties that bind our United Kingdom. Our Union', he says, 'is the most successful political and economic union in history. We are a global brand and together we are safer, stronger and more prosperous'. In what appears to be in contradiction to Michael Gove's claims yesterday, the Prime Minister tells reporters that he stands by his estimate during the Tory leadership campaign that the chances of leaving without an agreement are 'a million to one', and says his 'assumption is that we can get a new deal'.

Later in the day, the Prime Minister is booed by protestors in Edinburgh as he arrives for talks with Scotland's First Minister, Nicola Sturgeon. After reiterating to her that the UK would leave the EU on 31st October 'come what may' Mrs Sturgeon retaliates by describing Johnson's government as 'dangerous' and 'driving the country to disaster', adding, 'I think that this is a Government that is pursuing a no deal strategy, however much they may deny that in public'. The First Minister goes on to repeat her assertion that she would demand a second independence referendum for Scotland if the Prime Minister presses ahead with a no deal Brexit.

The financial markets do not seem impressed by the Prime Minister's firm stance on Brexit. At the end of the day, the pound is trading at 1.22 US dollars and 1.10 Euros, its lowest levels in two years and a fall of over 1% on the day.

Tuesday 30th July 2019

93 days to Brexit

The Prime Minister's roadshow reaches Wales today, with Boris Johnson holding talks with Wale's First Minister Mark Drakeford. Afterwards, Mr Drakeford claims that there was a 'deeply concerning lack of detail' from the Prime Minister regarding Brexit, adding that when he had pressed him to explain the path to a deal with the EU, he did not get a 'clear sense' of what the plan was.

Earlier in the day, reacting to concerns that a no deal Brexit would be detrimental to farmers, Welsh Secretary Alun Cairns suggests that new global markets, including Japan, will be available to lamb producers. Speaking to the BBC, Mr Cairns says, 'we are now looking to the growth that will come from right around the world, 90% of global growth will come from outside of the EU'. However, Plaid Cymru Westminster leader, Liz Saville Roberts, points out later, via Twitter, that the Japanese market has already been opened up to Welsh lamb by the EU-Japan trade deal.

During a day that also contains a flying visit to Brecon, the scene of an impending by-election in two days' time, the Prime Minister finally finds time, almost a week after his accession to the role, to speak with Irish Taoiseach Leo Varadkar. During the call, Boris Johnson assures him that the UK would 'never' erect a permanent border with Ireland but reinforces the message he gave to Nicola Sturgeon yesterday, insisting that the UK will leave the EU 'come what may' on 31st October. The Irish Prime Minister invites his counterpart to Dublin, but reiterates that the Withdrawal Agreement will not be reopened, and any deal must include the 'necessary' backstop.

Later in the evening, the Prime Minister travels to Northern Ireland where he dines with members of the Democratic Unionist Party and discusses the renewal of the supply deal agreement with the party at Westminster. Ahead of talks with the five main political parties tomorrow regarding the reviving of Stormont, Sinn Fein calls on the Irish Government to prepare for unification, their leader, Mary Lou McDonald, telling supporters in Belfast that Boris Johnson was 'not my Prime Minister'.

Meanwhile, back on the mainland, Brexit Party leader, Nigel Farage, slams Dominic Cummings as 'untrustworthy'. Speaking to 'The Times' newspaper, Mr Farage claims that the Prime Minister's chief advisor viewed Brexiteers as 'cretins and members of the lower order', adding that 'he has huge personal enmity with the true believers in Brexit'.

Wednesday 31st July 2019

92 days to Brexit

Ireland's Prime Minister Leo Varadkar again rejects calls for the Withdrawal Agreement to be reopened, saying Ireland 'isn't going to be bullied on this issue' as it had 'total support' from other EU countries.

Following talks the previous evening, Jeffrey Donaldson of the DUP signals his party's support for Boris Johnson's stance on Brexit. Talking to BBC Radio he states that the party agree with Johnson's assertion that the only way to get a Brexit deal through Parliament was to drop the Irish backstop, saying, 'I think given the response of the Irish government in particular, who I believe are key to this issue of addressing UK concerns about the backstop, I think the prospect of a no deal is significant'. His party leader, Arlene Foster, weighs in too, accusing the Taoiseach of engaging in 'project fear mark 2', and insisting that the Irish Prime Minister 'dial down the rhetoric' and 'engage' to 'find a way forward'.

During bilateral talks at Stormont Mary Lou McDonald, the leader of Sinn Fein, tells Boris Johnson that a failure to hold a vote on Irish reunification in the event of a no deal Brexit is 'unthinkable', claiming that, under the terms of the Good Friday Agreement of 1998, the incumbent Northern Ireland Secretary is obliged to enable a referendum on ending partition if there is evidence of a shift of public opinion in favour of Irish unity. A no deal Brexit, she claims, would be just such evidence.

Given that today is the by-election in Brecon and Radnorshire, there is a hiatus on political announcements domestically. The opinion polls are correct and the seat, currently held by the Conservatives, is taken by the Liberal Democrats, their candidate, Jane Dodds, taking 43% of the vote. The defeat reduces Boris Johnson's parliamentary majority to just one, including the DUP, and is a victory for a pro-remain alliance that saw other like-minded parties standing aside to offer the electorate of the Welsh constituency a single anti-Brexit candidate. The Conservative candidate, Chris Davis, captured 39 percent of the vote, fighting to retain the seat after being convicted and fined for expenses fraud, whilst the Brexit Party candidate came third with 10 percent. The Labour Party just about manage to hold on to their deposit, polling at a little over 5 percent.

There is more bad news for the Prime Minister this evening. Tory MP Dr Phillip Lee declares that he is to spend the summer recess considering whether he should defect to the Liberal Democrats. Dr Lee, who openly supports a second referendum, reveals in a podcast that he is 'really not comfortable about my party pushing for no deal Brexit without the proper consent of the public'. Should Dr Lee make the decision to defect, it would wipe out the Prime Minister's majority in the House of Commons.

A report by the British Chamber of Commerce in Germany, which represents companies in both countries, claims that a no deal Brexit would lead to thousands of job losses and cost Germany 1 percent of its GDP. The report shows manufacturing activity declining in France, Italy and Spain, with the Chamber's co-chairman, Alex Altmann, suggesting that 'a seven-year low manufacturing output is moving Germany, as the largest European economy, further into a risk of recession'. He concludes that 'a no deal Brexit with customs barriers, regulatory diversion and uncertainty around immigration will cost the German economy around 1 per cent of GDP with the potential of 200,000 job losses in the UK and Germany'.

In his most bizarre Brexit interjection to date, Labour peer Lord Adonis attracts criticism from all quarters, including his own party, when he tweets, in response to the Treasury announcing £2.1 billion for no deal funding, 'Mum, you know when I told you in March I was going to slash my wrists if you didn't do what I said. THIS TIME I REALLY MEAN IT. Just you watch.' His comments are condemned by the Shadow Minister for Mental Health who replies that his tweet was 'entirely inappropriate and in very poor taste'.

The Conservative Party Chairman, James Cleverly, hits the airwaves this morning, expressing his 'disappointment' at the outcome in the Brecon and Radnorshire by-election and declaring it the result of a 'dirty deal' with the Green Party and Plaid Cymru. Mr Cleverly points out that although the Brexit Party only achieved 10 percent of the vote, those votes, if combined with the Tories, would have been enough to deliver victory. He goes on to add that 'it is becoming obvious to all now that the Brexit Party standing against the Conservative Party would produce a massive own goal'. Allies of Nigel Farage are quick to leap on the comments, warning that the Prime Minister must start 'talking' to The Brexit Party.

The Governor of the Bank of England, Mark Carney, suggests that some major industries could become unviable if Britain leaves the EU without a deal. Accepting that no deal was now a 'significant possibility' Carney tells the BBC that 'the economics of no deal are that the rules of the game for exporting to Europe or importing from Europe fundamentally change', adding that, 'there are some very big industries in this country where that which is highly profitable becomes not profitable, becomes uneconomic'. Amongst those affected, he claims, will be the automotive, food, transport and chemical sectors. In response to the Governor's claims, former Conservative Party leader Iain Duncan Smith tells the 'Daily Telegraph' that Mark Carney was 'one of the architects and promoters of Project Fear'.

As is often the case with Saturdays, it is a slow news day politically, with interested parties keen to keep their powder dry for the 'big guns' of the Sunday press. It is announced, however, that the Prime Minister intends to pledge a £1.8 billion cash injection for the NHS, funding that, it is said, will be in addition to the £33.9 billion a year increase by 2023/24 that has already been promised by Theresa May. Response to the announcement is less than enthusiastic, the Labour Party claiming that it 'falls significantly short' of the amount needed to reverse Tory cuts and Liberal Democrat health spokeswoman, Baroness Jolly, declaring that the Prime Minister's pledge 'will not be worth the paper it's written on' when a no deal Brexit hits.

The leader of the SNP in Westminster, Ian Blackford, urges his counterparts in the opposition parties to join him in a cross-party summit to stop a no deal Brexit. In a letter to Labour's Jeremy Corbyn, Plaid Cymru's Liz Saville Roberts, the Liberal Democrats' Jo Swinson, Caroline Lucas from the Greens and Anna Soubry from the Independent Group for Change, Blackford says, 'time is short and we must act to prevent the Prime Minister destroying the futures of citizens up and down the country', calling on them to 'coalesce against a no deal Brexit' and the 'unmitigated damage' it will cause.

Sunday 4th August 2019

88 days to Brexit

It is revealed in today's 'Sunday Telegraph' that Boris Johnson's senior advisor, Dominic Cummings, told officials at a meeting last week that, even if rebel Tories and Labour MPs force a General Election after a vote of no confidence, it will be too late to prevent a no deal Brexit. 'If there is a no-confidence vote in September or October, we'll call an election for after the 31st and we'll leave anyway', Cummings is reported to have said. In response, former Attorney General, Dominic Grieve, conceded that Cummings has a point, but tells the BBC that 'there are a number of things the House of Commons can do, including bringing down the Government and setting up a new one in its place'. His comments are reinforced by Jonathan Ashworth, Labour health spokesman, who tells Sky News 'there will be opportunities for us when Parliament returns in September to stop no deal'.

In a letter to 'The Sunday Times' a group of 45 US Republican senators pledge to back a US/UK trade agreement even in the event of a no deal Brexit. The letter states that it is up to the UK Government to 'decide the terms of a Brexit deal with the EU. We will support whatever course Britain takes.' The letter goes on to say that 'if Britain leaves the EU with no deal, we will work with our administration, your government, and our friends in the EU to minimise disruptions in critical matters such as international air travel, financial transactions, and the shipment of medicine, food, and other vital supplies'. The show of support is in contrast to previous statements by Nancy Pelosi, the speaker of the US House of Representatives, who has warned that no trade deal would be agreed by Congress if Brexit in any way damages the Good Friday Agreement.

Writing for the 'Mail on Sunday', Brexit Secretary, Steve Barclay, argues that the European elections in May reconstituted the EU, meaning Michel Barnier's mandate to insist on the harsh terms of the Withdrawal Agreement was no longer valid. As a consequence, Barclay states that Barnier should go back to the leaders of the EU27 to change the terms of the talks. In response, Commission spokeswoman Mina Andreeva tells a news briefing in Brussels that, 'the Withdrawal Agreement is not up for negotiation but we are open to talks about the political declaration'. Later, diplomats from the EU's 27 other member states are briefed for two hours by European Commission official Stephanie Riso, a senior member of chief Brexit negotiator Michel Barnier's team. They are told to ramp up no deal preparations as the 'reality is sinking in' that both sides have run out of common ground, the diplomats concluding that Boris Johnson's Government had 'no intention' of negotiating in good faith and that his 'central scenario' is no deal.

Monday 5th August 2019

87 days to Brexit

Former Supreme Court Judge Lord Sumption tells the BBC Radio 4 'Today' programme that the Prime Minister did have discretion on setting election dates. 'It is not an unlimited discretion, but I cannot see how the courts could say the PM was not entitled to take political risks into consideration', he says. His comments come in response to press rumours over the weekend that, if he lost a vote of confidence in the Commons, Boris Johnson would refuse to leave Downing Street and would, instead, trigger a General Election for after the Brexit date of October 31st, preventing MPs from stopping the process.

A Downing Street spokeswoman reiterates that 'the Prime Minister wants to meet EU leaders and negotiate a new deal, one that abolishes the anti-democratic backstop. We will throw ourselves into the negotiations with the greatest energy and the spirit of friendship and we hope the EU will rethink its current refusal to make any changes to the Withdrawal Agreement. The fact is the Withdrawal Agreement has been rejected by Parliament three times and will not pass in its current form so if the EU wants a deal, it needs to change its stance. Until then, we will continue to prepare to leave the EU on October 31st'.

Tuesday 6th August 2019

86 days to Brexit

As Boris Johnson entertains the Estonian Prime Minister, Juri Ratas, in Downing Street, Michael Gove takes to the airwaves to tell Sky News, 'I'm deeply saddened that the EU now seem to be refusing to negotiate with the UK. The Prime Minister has been clear, he wants to negotiate a good deal with the European Union and he will apply all the energy of the Government and ensure that in a spirit of friendliness we can negotiate a new deal. But one thing is clear, the old deal that was negotiated has failed to pass the House of Commons three times now, so we do need a new approach. And whatever happens, while we remain ready and willing to negotiate, the EU must appreciate we are leaving on October 31st, deal or no deal'.

Later, on a visit to Hillsborough Castle in Northern Ireland, the Irish Prime Minister, Leo Varadkar, reiterates the EU position that the Withdrawal Agreement was not open for renegotiation, but he insists there is scope to offer clarifications on the deal and make changes to the Political Declaration on the future relationship. 'I don't accept it's unavoidable', he says of the prospects of no deal. 'There are many ways by which a no deal can be avoided. Either by the ratification of the Withdrawal Agreement, a further extension or revocation of Article 50. So, there are a number of ways that a no deal can be avoided on the 31st of October. I am certainly not fatalistic about that'.

Foreign Secretary Dominic Raab begins a three-day trip to Canada, North America and Mexico. Meeting with his Canadian counterpart, Chrystia Freeland, in Toronto he says that the UK is at 'an important historic crossroads' and 'we need to ensure everything possible is in place to provide continuity of trade after Brexit, for the benefit of companies and consumers in both our countries and indeed wider countries around the world'. He concludes by saying, 'as part of that we want to take our friendship with Canada and the Canadian people to the next level on trade, on security cooperation, on human rights and on those global challenges which are beyond any particular region'.

At the Edinburgh Fringe Festival, during an onstage interview, Shadow Chancellor, John McDonnell, says that any decision on holding a second referendum on independence was a matter for the Scottish Parliament. He tells broadcaster Iain Dale, 'it will be for the Scottish Parliament and the Scottish people to decide that. They will take a view about whether they want another referendum'.

The Shadow Chancellor's comments last night at the Edinburgh Fringe have created a storm of controversy, his words being seen by some as a means to pave the way for an electoral pact with the SNP after Nicola Sturgeon had earlier floated the idea of a 'progressive alliance' with Jeremy Corbyn to 'lock the Tories out of government' and 'stop Brexit'. Former Scottish Secretary, Douglas Alexander, declares the remarks 'strikingly ignorant', while Scottish Conservative Leader, Ruth Davidson, points out that a 'once in a generation' vote had been held in 2014. 'Jeremy Corbyn and John McDonnell would happily sell Scotland down the river if they thought it could give them a sniff of power', she adds. Labour MP for Edinburgh South, Ian Murray, also attacks the Shadow Chancellor, saying 'these are utterly irresponsible comments from John McDonnell that betray our party's values', while Labour MP John Mann says Mr McDonnell had 'dumped on' the party's Scottish wing.

Boris Johnson will 'trigger the biggest constitutional crisis since Charles I was beheaded' says Tory grandee Sir Malcolm Rifkind in response to clams that, if defeated in a vote of no confidence, the Prime Minister would refuse to resign and simply trigger a General Election. In a letter to 'The Times' Sir Malcolm adds, 'if the Prime Minister refused to respect the normal consequence of losing a confidence vote and if he sought to prevent both Parliament and the electorate having a final say on no deal, he would create the gravest constitutional crisis since the actions of Charles I led to the Civil War'. His comments are echoed by former Attorney General, Dominic Grieve, who claims that 'the Queen would have to sack him. She is the ultimate guardian of our constitution. That's her job'. Gina Miller, the businesswoman and campaigner who went to court to win the right for Parliament to give its consent ahead of the Government triggering Article 50 also agrees, telling BBC Radio 4, 'there is a solid convention that a Prime Minister losing a vote of no confidence must step down'.

Dominic Raab moves on to Washington to meet Donald Trump and Vice President Mike Pence, hailing the President's 'warmth and enthusiasm for the UK-US relationship' and declaring that 'the UK looks forward to working with our American friends to reach a free trade deal that is good for both countries, and cooperating on the common security challenges we face'.

Having earlier been dismissed by Dominic Grieve as 'arrogant', Dominic Cummings is door-stepped by Sky News, the Prime Minister's senior advisor telling the station that 'the Prime Minister believes politicians don't get to choose which votes they respect'.

The Food and Drink Federation calls on the government to change competition law to allow them to stockpile enough food for Christmas in the event of a no deal Brexit. The FDF's chief operating officer, Tim Rycroft, believes that shortages of some foods could go on for 'weeks or months', potentially meaning it could spill over into the festive period. 'In the event of no deal disruption', he tells the BBC, 'if the Government wants the food supply chain to work together to tackle likely shortages, to decide where to prioritise shipments, they will have to provide cast-iron written reassurances that competition law will not be strictly applied to those discussions'. His request is rebuffed by Michael Gove, who insists that the 'resilient' UK food sector would be able to cope in the event of no deal.

Dominic Rabb visits Mexico, hailing a 'win-win' relationship with the country as he announces that the UK will provide £60 million to help tackle poverty and corruption and open the country up to British businesses. As he signs the agreement, the Foreign Secretary declares it as 'the most wide-ranging agreement ever concluded' between the two countries which will see them work closely together on trade, investment and climate change. Mr Raab also goes on to say that if Brussels does not show flexibility on amending the terms of Britain's withdrawal from the European Union, it will have to take responsibility for a no deal scenario.

Two weeks after taking over as Prime Minister, Boris Johnson has led his party to a nine-point lead over Labour according to a YouGov poll of General Election voting intentions released today. In what has been dubbed the 'Boris bounce' the poll puts the Conservative Party on 33 percent, with Labour on 22. The Liberal Democrats have risen two points, from 19 to 21 percent under new leader Jo Swinson, whilst the Brexit Party have also risen one point, to 14 percent.

The Prime Minister announces that he is to scrap immigration caps on leading figures from science, medicine, engineering and the arts who want to come to work in the UK. In a live Facebook broadcast from Downing Street he says that, 'we have to not only support the talent that we already have here, but also ensure our immigration system attracts the very best minds from around the world'.

The Labour Leader, Jeremy Corbyn, writes to Cabinet Secretary, Sir Mark Sedwill, insisting that Boris Johnson should be blocked from taking Britain out of the EU during a General Election campaign. His letter comes in response to claims from allies of the Prime Minister that, if he was defeated in a vote of no confidence, he would call a General Election for early November, allowing Brexit to happen automatically. Mr Corbyn's letter goes on to say that should the Prime Minister follow such a course it would be an 'unprecedented, unconstitutional and an anti-democratic abuse of power', adding that election rules made it clear that policy decisions on which a new government 'might be expected to want to take a different view' should be postponed until after polling day.

A fast track spending review is ordered by the Chancellor of the Exchequer, Sajid Javid, sparking speculation that the Government is preparing for a General Election. Civil servants are ordered to provide a one year spending round, contradicting the usual process of departments bidding for their budgets for the next five years. Announcing the move, the Chancellor says, 'we will get Brexit done by October 31st and put our country on the road to a brighter future. The Prime Minister and I have asked for a fast-tracked spending round for September to set departmental budgets for next year. This will clear the ground ahead of Brexit while delivering on people's priorities'.

Figures released today by the Office for National Statistics show that the UK's economy shrank for the first time since 2012 in the second quarter of this year, as the manufacturing and construction sectors both declined. Gross Domestic Product decreased by 0.2% in the period between April and June, but Chancellor of the Exchequer, Sajid Javid, says he is not expecting a recession, and that the reason for the 'volatility' was uncertainty about Brexit, which could be resolved by leaving the EU on October 31st. 'I'm not expecting a recession, there is not a single leading forecaster out there that is expecting a recession, the independent Bank of England is not expecting a recession', Javid tells Channel 4 news, adding 'our economy remains strong and we are actually, in terms of fundamentals, one of the strongest economies in the developed world'.

Transport Minister George Freeman incurs the wrath of Downing Street by warning that a no deal Brexit would be an 'absolute disaster' and that failure to reach an agreement would be so chaotic it could keep the Tories out of power for decades. Freeman also claims that dissolving Parliament for an election after the Brexit date would be a 'huge mistake'. Following a rebuke from the Prime Minister he later backtracks, releasing a statement saying, 'the PM has repeatedly set out his desire for a deal and our willingness to negotiate with all energy, but if the Commission is unwilling to negotiate, then we will still leave on October 31st. I firmly support the Prime Minister and his approach'.

Saturday 10th August 2019

82 days to Brexit

The UK may struggle to patrol its own fishing waters after a no deal Brexit, a government email reveals. The memo, written by the Department of the Environment, Fisheries and Rural Affairs (DEFRA) officials, which was accidentally sent to the BBC, claims there is 'a lot of uncertainty' over whether Britain has the resources to police its seas should it leave the Common Fisheries Policy and become an independent coastal state under a no deal Brexit. The document raises concerns that only 12 vessels will be available 'to monitor a space three times the size of the surface area of the UK'.

Jean-Claude Juncker, the President of the European Commission, warns that Britain will come off worst in a no deal Brexit. The EU president tells the Austrian newspaper Tiroler Tageszeitung, 'if it comes to a hard Brexit, this is in no one's interest, but the British would be the big losers. They pretend it's not like that, but it will be. We have made it clear that we are unwilling to renegotiate the exit agreement'.

Richard Braine is elected leader of the UK Independence Party (UKIP) with 53% of the party vote. Braine takes over from Gerard Batten who stood down after the European elections.

Sunday 11th August 2019

81 days to Brexit

In a series of announcements over the weekend, suggested by many to be part of a surreptitious election campaign, Boris Johnson vows to 'come down hard' on crime, promising a £2.5 billion programme to create 10,000 additional prison places along with the extension of enhanced stop-and-search powers for police forces across England and Wales.

The head of the French channel ports dismisses fears of no deal Brexit chaos at Dover or Calais, praising the 'highly professional' UK preparations. Jean-Marc Puissesseau, President of Port Boulogne Calais, plays down concerns about preparations, saying 'nothing is going to happen the day after Brexit. Britain will be a third country, that's all, and there is no reason why this should lead to any problems.'

The 'Sunday Telegraph' reports that the Prime Minister has accepted an offer from Irish premier Leo Varadkar to meet to try to break the Brexit deadlock. However, the Irish Government later insists that the backstop will not be up for renegotiation. A spokesman for the Taoiseach confirms that the leaders are 'in contact to agree a date for these talks in the coming weeks', but adds, 'as has repeatedly been made clear, the Withdrawal Agreement and the backstop are not up for negotiation'.

The 'Boris bounce' may not as robust as previously suggested. A YouGov poll of 1,200 voters, in 20 constituencies with small Tory leads and where the Lib Dems came second in 2017, shows a 14 percent slump for the Conservatives.

Monday 12th August 2019

80 days to Brexit

Boris Johnson and Donald Trump speak for the third time in three weeks, with Downing Street revealing that the leaders discussed global economic issues, trade and Brexit.

Writing in 'The Guardian', Green Party leader Caroline Lucas suggests that the way to avoid a no deal Brexit is for Parliament to pass a vote of no-confidence in the Government, and then for an all-female emergency Cabinet to take over. She writes that women 'have shown they can bring a different perspective to crises, are able to reach out to those they disagree with and cooperate to find solutions', adding that they are less 'tribal' than men and more prepared to compromise. Her idea is roundly rejected, with Diane Abbott, the shadow Home Secretary, describing the idea, in a tweet, as a 'backdoor route to a National Government', saying 'whatever the gender of the participants' it 'won't work'. Lucas also attracts criticism for the fact that her list of suggested participants in the emergency cabinet are all white, something for which she later apologises saying she was 'wrong to overlook' her 'women of colour colleagues'.

Donald Trump's Security Adviser, John Bolton, arrives in London for two days of talks. After meeting with Boris Johnson in Downing Street he urges British officials to 'get Brexit done' saying that the UK will be 'first in line' for a trade deal with the US whether or not a Brexit deal is secured.

Speaking at an event at the Edinburgh Fringe, The Speaker of the House of Commons insists that the Prime Minister would not 'get away' with attempting to prorogue Parliament. 'The one thing I feel strongly about is that the House of Commons must have its way', he says, 'and if there is an attempt to circumvent, to bypass or, God forbid, to close down Parliament, that is anathema to me. I will fight with every breath in my body to stop that happening. We cannot have a situation in which Parliament is shut down. We are a democratic society and Parliament will be heard'.

Also in Edinburgh today, a court battle is launched to stop Boris Johnson suspending Parliament. Over 70 MPs and peers urge the Court of Session to rule that proroguing Parliament to ensure the UK leaves the EU without a deal is unlawful and unconstitutional. A hearing is scheduled for September 6th at the Edinburgh court.

John Bolton holds talks with the Chancellor, Sajid Javid, and Liz Truss, the Business Secretary, the discussion, according to a Washington official, focussing on 'a partial trade agreement that could come into effect on November 1st if Brexit takes place as scheduled'.

Jeremy Corbyn must work with the Liberal Democrats to stop a no deal Brexit, his deputy warns. Tom Watson, speaking alongside Jo Swinson at an event hosted by young campaigners for staying in the EU, says that party allegiances needed to be set aside to obstruct Boris Johnson's Brexit plans. 'Everyone who cares about democracy, our country and our future must work together', he says, 'because there are enough of us, from all parties in Parliament, to stop him'.

In an article for 'The Times' newspaper, former Chancellor of the Exchequer, Philip Hammond, takes a swipe at the Prime Minister's chief advisor, Dominic Cummings, referring to 'the unelected people who pull the strings of this government' making demands that 'the EU cannot, and will not, accede to'. Hammond goes on to say that the suggestion that leave voters were told of the risks of a no deal exit is 'a total travesty of the truth', warning that a no deal Brexit will cost jobs, lead to a decline in living standards and risk breaking up the Union, reducing the UK to an 'inward-looking little England'. He concludes by declaring that 'no deal would be a betrayal of the 2016 referendum result. It must not happen'. In response to his column, a senior Downing Street source is reported as saying 'everyone knows that the ex-chancellor's real objective was to cancel the referendum result'.

The Labour Party Leader, Jeremy Corbyn, writes a letter to opposition party leaders, and some rebel Tory MPs, offering to lead a 'strictly time-limited' government to secure an extension to Article 50. Corbyn asks for their support with a Commons vote of no confidence, and says that he would then stop no deal before calling a general election and campaigning for a new referendum. Liberal Democrat leader, Jo Swinson, rejects the idea out of hand, saying it was a 'nonsense' and not a 'serious attempt' to stop no deal, while former Conservative Party Leader, Iain Duncan Smith, says, 'Corbyn realises he isn't going to win the vote of confidence because no other party trusts him. He is desperate to win the vote and this is him in a panic'.

The Prime Minister takes to Facebook once again, this time to hold a first ever 'People's PMQs'. In response to a question about parliamentary opposition to Brexit, Boris Johnson replies, 'there is a terrible kind of collaboration going on between people who think they can block Brexit in Parliament and our European friends'. The PM also answers questions on mental health, knife crime and the Union in a broadcast that lasts 12 minutes and is watched by over 7,000 people at its peak.

Jeremy Corbyn's letter continues to provoke reaction, with Conservative backbencher Guto Bebb taking to the airwaves to urge Tory rebels and others to 'take seriously' the offer from the Labour leader to become caretaker Prime Minister. He tells the BBC, 'I think there are other proposals that can be taken in terms of ensuring that no deal is taken off the table. But I certainly take the view that a short-term Jeremy Corbyn government is less damaging than the generational damage that would be caused by a no deal Brexit'. The SNP's leader in Westminster, Ian Blackford, insists that his party's priority was to stop no deal, not install Mr Corbyn in Downing Street, whilst Anna Soubry, the leader of the Independent Group for Change, says she could not make Mr Corbyn Prime Minister 'for all manner of reasons'. Jo Swinson expands on her initial rebuttal of Corbyn's proposal saying 'what we need in a leader of an emergency government is a long-serving Member of Parliament who is respected on both sides of the House. Someone like Ken Clarke or Harriet Harman'.

Three Conservative MPs who were copied in on Mr Corbyn's letter, Dominic Grieve, Dame Caroline Spelman and Sir Oliver Letwin are reported to have sent a written response to the Labour leader saying 'we agree that our common priority should be to work together in Parliament to prevent no deal Brexit and welcome your invitation to discuss the different ways that this might be achieved. We would be happy to meet with you as well as colleagues from other opposition parties whenever convenient in the weeks before Parliament returns.' Responding to the news, Transport Secretary Grant Shapps says it was 'absolutely extraordinary' that any Conservatives would even consider helping the leader of the opposition into Downing Street.

In what appears to confirm John McDonnell's comments at the Edinburgh Fringe, Jeremy Corbyn says that he does not believe a second referendum on Scotland leaving the UK would be a good idea and he would advise against holding one, but he insists MPs in Westminster should not stand in the way if Scotland wanted another public vote on the issue. Scottish Conservatives immediately accuse Mr Corbyn of 'surrendering' to Nicola Sturgeon in a bid to secure SNP support for a future Labour-led government.

Ken Clarke says that he would be willing to become caretaker Prime Minister to stop Britain leaving the EU without a deal on October 31st. Speaking on Radio 4's 'PM' programme he comments, "if it was the only way in which the plain majority in the House of Commons that is opposed to a no deal exit could find a way forward, I actually said to Jo (Swinson) when she managed to raise me when I was on holiday that I wouldn't object to it, if that was in the judgment of people, the only way forward'. His suggestion is met with a stinging rebuke from Nigel Evans, a member of the 1922 committee of Tory MPs, who told the same programme, 'we've filled the vacancy with Boris Johnson and so I really don't know what Ken is talking about. It does seem to be Westminster meets La La Land because it's not as if these ideas are half-baked, I really don't think they've been anywhere near an oven'. Asked by the BBC if he would back Harriet Harman or Ken Clarke to be an interim Prime Minister, Jeremy Corbyn says, 'we are putting forward the Labour position and I am the leader of the Labour Party to do just that. It's not up to Jo Swinson to choose candidates,' he adds, 'it's not up to Jo Swinson to decide who the next Prime Minister is going to be'.

Liberal Democrat leader Jo Swinson tweets, 'I've offered to meet Jeremy Corbyn to discuss how we can work together on a deliverable plan to stop no deal, including the option of uniting behind an MP who can command a majority in the House'. Two of the Tory rebels who were included on the circulation list for Corbyn's letter also issue clarifications. Dame Caroline Spelman says that while she is happy to work with Mr Corbyn on options such as changing the law to block no deal, she would not vote to bring down the government in a confidence vote, and Dominic Grieve says in a leaked email that and he would not do anything to 'facilitate Jeremy Corbyn's arrival in Downing Street'.

Former Chancellor Philip Hammond is facing the prospect of a vote of no confidence in his Surrey constituency following his newspaper column, and subsequent media appearances, denouncing a no deal Brexit. Party insiders tell 'The Telegraph' that local activists were 'not best pleased' at Mr Hammond working against Mr Johnson and there was 'no doubt' that tensions would boil over in the near future.

Saturday 17th August 2019

75 days to Brexit

Leaked Whitehall papers suggest that the UK faces three months of chaos at the ports as well as fuel, medicine and food shortages in the event of a no deal Brexit. Operation Yellowhammer, a secret dossier filed by the Cabinet Office, says that massive tailbacks at ports could limit fuel distribution and up to 85% of lorries heading to France could be caught in delays. Fresh food supply will plummet, the report adds, leading to increased prices and less variety, while medical supplies will also be vulnerable to severe extended delays.

Boris Johnson, in a letter to former Chancellor Philip Hammond and his co-plotters says, 'the EU can see the public debate among Parliamentarians and they have been told privately by some British politicians that Parliament will frustrate our exit on 31st October. Some of you have said publicly that you are determined to try to stop us leaving the EU on that date if we cannot secure a deal'. He goes on to say, 'it is as plain as a pikestaff that Brussels, or the EU 27, will simply not compromise as long as they believe there is the faintest possibility that Parliament can block Brexit on 31st October', warning that, 'the so-called efforts to prevent no deal are in fact making no deal more likely' as it was giving Brussels a false sense of hope that the UK will climb down.

Despite the idea being rejected by the Liberal Democrats and a number of Conservative rebels, Labour leader Jeremy Corbyn insists that he should be installed as the caretaker Prime Minister in the event of Boris Johnson losing a vote of confidence. Speaking on a visit to Bolton, Mr Corbyn says, 'what we need is a respect for the electoral process that brought about the results from the last general election', adding, 'we will do everything we can to stop a no deal Brexit. I am the leader of the Labour Party, Labour is the largest opposition party by far. That is the process that must be followed'.

Sunday 18th August 2019

74 days to Brexit

The blame for yesterday's leak of the Operation Yellowhammer document is attributed to former Cabinet ministers, with Downing Street saying the report is 'from when ministers were blocking what needed to be done to get ready to leave and the funds were not available' and 'has been deliberately leaked by a former minister in an attempt to influence discussions with EU leaders'. Michael Gove later adds, 'this is an old document. Since it was published and circulated, the Government has taken significant steps to ensure that we are prepared to leave on October 31st, deal or no deal'.

In a letter to Boris Johnson, 100 backbench MPs demand that the summer parliamentary recess be cancelled, along with the planned three-week break for the party conference season. They write, 'Parliament must be recalled now and sit until October 31st, so that the voices of the people can be heard and there is proper scrutiny of your Government. At times of grave economic emergency and threats to our national security, Parliament has been recalled to allow MPs to make representations and to hold ministers to account'. In response, Energy Minister, Kwasi Kwarteng, tells Sky News that the recess dates have been agreed by the Commons and there would be plenty of time to discuss Brexit next month.

Monday 19th August 2019

73 days to Brexit

In a letter to the European Council President, Donald Tusk, Boris Johnson says that the Irish backstop is 'anti-democratic', 'unviable' and 'unsustainable' as the basis for a long-term relationship, adding that it also puts the Good Friday Agreement at risk. He goes on to say that Britain and the EU should commit to finding 'alternative arrangements' to manage the Irish border by the end of a transition period. He concludes by saying that 'the backstop cannot form part of an agreed Withdrawal Agreement. That is a fact we must both acknowledge. I believe the task before us is to strive to find other solutions, and I believe an agreement is possible'. Within hours, Donald Tusk replies, saying that anyone opposing the backstop without a 'realistic' plan was actually 'supporting the reestablishment of a border' because there was currently no alternative.

In a speech in Corby, Jeremy Corbyn urges MPs to support his proposal to oust Boris Johnson and help him form a temporary government with the single goal of delaying Brexit beyond October 31st. The Labour leader warns that the UK is heading for a 'political and constitutional storm' and says that his party would do 'everything necessary' to stop a no deal split from the EU. 'I will bring a vote of no confidence in the government, and if we're successful, I would seek to form a time-limited caretaker administration to avert no deal' he vows but, when questioned by journalists he refuses to say whether he would back another candidate to be the temporary Prime Minister if he was unable to win majority support in the House of Commons.

Senate Democratic leader Chuck Schumer warns, in a letter to US Secretary of State Mike Pompeo, that Congress could work on a cross-party basis to block a post Brexit trade deal with the UK if a hard border is introduced on the island of Ireland. 'While Britain is a unique and valued ally of our nation', he says, 'I write to express my inveterate opposition to any prospective trade deal with the UK that either undermines the landmark Good Friday Agreement or facilitates a return to a hard border'.

The UK government tells the EU that British officials will stop attending most meetings from September 1st to free up time to work on Brexit. The Department for Exiting the European Union says UK officials will now attend only the meetings that 'really matter' of more than 800 scheduled, with Brexit Secretary, Steve Barclay, adding that the move would free up 'hundreds of hours' to 'get on with preparing for our departure on October 31st and seizing the opportunities that lie ahead'.

In an interview with ITV News, Boris Johnson says, 'I saw what Donald Tusk had to say and it wasn't relevant of a sense of optimism. But I think actually we will get there', adding that he believes there are 'plenty of other creative solutions' to the Northern Irish backstop. The Prime Minister goes on to say, 'I think it's a bit paradoxical that the EU side is talking about us putting up all the barriers, we've made it clear 1,000 times we don't want to see any checks on the Northern Irish frontier at all, under no circumstances let me repeat again, under no circumstances will the Government of the United Kingdom be putting checks on the Northern Irish frontier. By contrast, it is the EU who currently claim that the single market and the plurality of the single market require them to have such checks. I don't think that's true'.

Boris Johnson travels to Berlin for talks with the German Chancellor Angela Merkel. After their meeting, Mrs Merkel suggests that ditching the Irish backstop was possible if the UK can come up with practical and workable alternatives within the next 30 days. She insists that Germany is ready for a no deal Brexit, but adds that if the UK could solve the 'conundrum' of the Irish border protocol she would be willing to listen to the proposals. In response, Boris Johnson welcomes what he describes as a 'blistering timetable', agreeing that the 'onus is on us to produce those solutions'.

Simon Coveney, the Irish Foreign Affairs Minister, says that while no one wanted to see the relationship between Ireland and the UK deteriorate, Dublin would not be 'steam-rolled' by London. 'We are not in the business of being steam-rolled at the end of this because a British Prime Minister has rolled out new red lines. That's not a reasonable approach', he says, adding, 'if we didn't have the backstop, we wouldn't have answers to how we solve the border challenge'.

In another letter to opposition party leaders and rebel Tory MPs, Jeremy Corbyn invites them to a meeting on 27th August. The letter says that 'it is vital that we meet urgently, before Parliament returns' describing the prospect of a no deal Brexit as 'real and threatening' and concluding that 'we must do everything we can to stop it'.

In a joint letter to the Prime Minister, 17 royal colleges and charities say they are 'simply unable to reassure patients' that their care will not be affected by a no deal Brexit, adding that, 'delays at our borders could exacerbate supply issues and create the very real possibility that life-saving medication and devices are delayed from making it into the UK'. They conclude by suggesting that Health Secretary Matt Hancock should be included on the No Deal Planning Committee to ensure that patient welfare is 'at the heart of Brexit negotiations.'

An opinion poll conducted by KantarTNS puts the Conservative Party on 42 per cent, 17 points higher than the company's last poll in May. The Labour Party are six points lower than last time, on 28 percent, while the Liberal Democrats remained on 15 percent, with the Brexit Party polling at 5 percent.

The Prime Minister meets Emmanuel Macron at the Elysee Palace, the French President adopting a similar line to that of Angela Merkel yesterday. 'We should together be able to find something smart within 30 days if there is goodwill on both sides', he says, but adds, 'we will not find a new withdrawal agreement within 30 days that will be very different from the existing one'. The Prime Minister praises the positive attitude of the German and French leaders, saying, 'where there's a will, there's a way'.

Julian Reichelt, the editor in chief of the German newspaper Bild, tells BBC Newsnight, 'I predict we will end up with something that's a no deal Brexit with so many side agreements, that it's basically a Brexit deal. That is the classic way of Angela Merkel, not giving in, but giving in'.

All of the Westminster opposition party leaders agree to meet Jeremy Corbyn for talks on how to prevent a no deal Brexit, but Jo Swinson, leader of the Liberal Democrats, warns in a tweet that she will be asking the Labour leader 'if he is open to all options'. Her comments are echoed by Liz Saville-Roberts, Plaid Cymru leader, who says, 'in this crisis, policy comes before personality. If Corbyn fails to offer a workable plan, others must be given the opportunity'.

Boris Johnson plays down some press reports claiming that, following his meetings with the German and French leaders, the prospect of a no deal Brexit has been lessened. Speaking on a visit to Devon, he concedes that the two leaders could 'see that we want a deal' and 'can see the problems with the backstop', but adds, 'I want to caution everybody, OK? Because this is not going to be a cinch, this is not going to be easy. We will have to work very hard to get this thing done. To persuade our EU friends and partners, who are very, very, very hard over against it, will take some time'. He goes on to warn that people should not 'get their hopes up too soon'.

The Prime Minister's talks in Europe seem to have bought him a little time with Tory rebel MPs, one telling 'The Times' newspaper that they would be reluctant to move against him before the 30 days are up. 'Tory MPs are not going to vote down the government while they think there's a potential deal to be done', the unnamed source says, adding, 'how would they justify that?'

David Davis, former Brexit Secretary, warns that concessions on the backstop alone may not be enough to get the Withdrawal Agreement past Parliament. Speaking to 'The Telegraph', Mr Davis says, 'I'd argue for contingency on the money. I'd argue for tighter limits, timetable limits, sunset clauses on the ECJ and things like that. I'd have a small shopping list'.

At a gathering of central bankers in the US, The Governor of the Bank of England, Mark Carney, warns that interest rates are 'more likely to ease than not' if Boris Johnson and EU officials fail to hammer out an agreement, arguing that 'in the event of a no deal, no transition brexit, sterling would probably fall, pushing up inflation, and demand would weaken further'.

Saturday 24th August 2019

68 days to Brexit

On the eve of a G7 meeting, European Council President, Donald Tusk, warns that he would not co-operate with the UK over a no deal Brexit, saying, 'I hope Prime Minister Johnson would not like to go down in history as Mr No Deal'. In response, Boris Johnson tells reporters, 'I don't want a no deal Brexit but I say to our friends in the EU, if they don't want a no deal Brexit then we've got to get rid of the backstop from the treaty'. He goes on to add, 'if Donald Tusk doesn't want to go down as Mr No Deal Brexit then I hope that point should be borne in mind by him too'.

Before the formal meeting of the G7 in Biarritz, Boris Johnson meets Donald Trump, with the US President hailing him 'the right man for the job', adding, 'we are going to do a very big trade deal, bigger than we have ever had with the UK'. Mr Trump describes the UK's membership of the EU as an 'anchor around their ankle' and suggests that a post Brexit trade deal between the two countries will be done 'pretty quickly'. For his part, Boris Johnson informs the US President that the NHS will be 'completely off limits' during post-Brexit trade talks, but says of the proposed deal, 'I'd love to do it within a year, but that's a very fast timetable'.

Ahead of talks with Donald Tusk, the Prime Minister says that striking an agreement with the EU is now just 'touch and go', adding that it 'all depends on our EU friends and partners'. During his meeting with the President of the European Council, Boris Johnson warns that Britain will not pay all of the £39 billion Brexit divorce bill if the UK has to leave the bloc without a deal on October 31st, suggesting that a figure of £9bn was more realistic under those circumstances. The Prime Minister says, 'if we come out without an agreement it is certainly true that the £39 billion is no longer, strictly speaking, owed'. After their meeting, an EU official declares that 'nothing substantive or new has emerged during the talks'.

Referring to the planned meeting on Tuesday between Jeremy Corbyn and Westminster opposition party leaders to discuss how to prevent a no deal Brexit, Barry Gardiner describes the Liberal Democrat leader, Jo Swinson, as 'petulant'. In an interview with Sky News, the shadow Trade Secretary goes on to say that the 'natural constitutional process' was that the leader of the opposition was called upon by the Queen to lead a new government when an old one failed.

In response to Boris Johnson's suggestion that the UK will not owe £39 billion in the event of a no deal Brexit, Guy Verhofstadt, the European Parliament's Brexit co-ordinator, says, 'if the UK doesn't pay what is due, the EU will not negotiate a trade deal', adding, 'after a no deal, this will be a first condition of any talks. Britain is better than this'.

At his press conference at the end of the G7 meeting in Biarritz, Boris Johnson insists that both he and the EU were keen to do a deal on Brexit. 'I think it's what the people want, I also think, by the way, it's what our friends and partners on the other side of the Channel want, they want it over', he says, adding, 'I do think that the EU does tend to come to an agreement right at the end'. The Prime Minister goes on to say that he is 'marginally more optimistic' about a deal, but adds that 'absolutely colossal and extensive' plans for a no deal will be in place should an agreement not be reached.

On the eve of his meeting with opposition party leaders in Westminster, Jeremy Corbyn declares that a no deal Brexit will only benefit the rich and reaffirms his intention to stop it. Writing in 'The Independent', the Labour leader says, 'the battle to stop no deal Brexit isn't a struggle between those who want to leave the EU and those who want continued membership. It's a battle of the many against the few who are hijacking the referendum result to shift even more power and wealth towards those at the top. That's why the Labour Party will do everything necessary to stop a no deal bankers' Brexit'.

Plans by Justin Welby, the Archbishop of Canterbury, to chair a citizens' assembly in which 100 people representing all sides of the argument would make recommendations on Brexit are criticised as being 'deeply inappropriate' by Iain Duncan Smith. 'I generally don't criticise the Archbishop but he shouldn't allow himself to be tempted into what is essentially a very political issue right now', the former Conservative Party leader says, adding that the idea was 'designed to destabilise Boris Johnson's position'.

The Brexit Party leader, Nigel Farage, addresses his 635 parliamentary candidates at a rally in London, telling then that a no deal Brexit is now 'the only acceptable deal'. He goes on to add that he would only agree to form a 'non-aggression pact' with Boris Johnson if the Tories switched to backing no deal, warning, 'if you sell us out on Brexit with this awful withdrawal treaty, we will fight you in every seat'.

Jeremy Corbyn meets opposition party leaders in Westminster and a statement, from all 6 leaders, is issued saying, 'the attendees agreed that Boris Johnson has shown himself open to using anti-democratic means to force through no deal. The attendees agreed on the urgency to act together to find practical ways to prevent no deal, including the possibility of passing legislation and a vote of no confidence'. Mr Corbyn went on to say, 'the motion of no confidence will be put, by me, at an appropriate time but obviously not the first item next Tuesday because I believe it's important we get on with a legislative process which prevents the Prime Minister acting in defiance of the will of Parliament'. It is later reported that in order to secure the agreement of the others, Jeremy Corbyn had to drop his preferred scheme to install himself as caretaker Prime Minister in the event of the Government losing a vote of no confidence.

Chancellor of the Exchequer, Sajid Javid, announces plans for an emergency budget on September 4th, sparking another round of rumours that the Government is plotting an early General Election. Writing in the 'Daily Telegraph', he says, 'thanks to the hard work of the British people over the last decade, we can afford to spend more on the people's priorities, without breaking the rules around what the Government should spend, and we'll do that in a few key areas like schools, hospitals and police'.

In a move that sparks fury across Westminster, Boris Johnson announces that he will dissolve Parliament in the second week of September. In a letter to MPs the Prime Minister says, 'This morning I spoke to Her Majesty The Queen to request an end to the current parliamentary session in the second sitting week in September, before commencing the second session of this Parliament with a Queen's speech on Monday 14th October. A central feature of the legislative programme will be the Government's number one legislative priority, if a new deal is forthcoming at EU Council, to introduce a Withdrawal Agreement Bill and move at pace to secure its passage before 31st October.' Labour MP Angela Eagle describes the action as a 'grubby manoeuvre' whilst the Labour Deputy Leader, Tom Watson, calls it an 'utterly scandalous affront to our democracy', adding, 'we must not let this happen'.

Jeremy Corbyn describes the move to dissolve Parliament as 'reckless', calling it 'an outrage and a threat to our democracy' whilst former Chancellor of the Exchequer, Philip Hammond, and the Speaker of the House of Commons, John Bercow, both describe it as 'a constitutional outrage'. The Speaker goes on to declare the plan to shut down Parliament from around September 11th until the state opening on October 14th was an 'offence against the democratic process'. SNP Westminster leader Ian Blackford tweets, 'Boris Johnson is acting like a dictator by attempting to shut down democracy to impose an extreme Brexit. He has no mandate, no majority, and he must be stopped. The SNP will be doing everything we can to stop Brexit and prevent a no deal disaster'. Conservative rebel Dominic Grieve says, of a vote of no confidence, that he would back one if necessary. 'I would wish, if at all possible, to avoid bringing down a Conservative government on a vote of no confidence', the MP for Beaconsfield says, 'but if that is what it ultimately took, I would be willing to do it. I think there are a number of colleagues who have said exactly the same thing'.

Boris Johnson says it is 'completely untrue' to suggest that Brexit was the reason for his decision to prorogue Parliament, insisting that he needed a Queen's Speech to set out a 'very exciting agenda' of domestic policy. 'There will be ample time on both sides of that crucial October 17th summit, ample time in Parliament for MPs to debate the EU, to debate Brexit, and all the other issues', the Prime Minister adds. The DUP release a statement saying that they support the decision to suspend Parliament but warn that the move would require a review of their confidence and supply arrangement with the Government.

Labour leader, Jeremy Corbyn, write to the Queen saying, 'there is a danger that the royal prerogative is being set directly against the wishes of a majority of the House of Commons. In the circumstances, as the leader of the official opposition, on behalf of all my party members and many other members of Parliament, I request you to grant me a meeting, along with other privy councillors, as a matter of urgency and before any final decision is taken'. Liberal Democrat leader Jo Swinson also writes to the monarch 'to express my concern at Boris Johnson's anti-democratic plan to shut down Parliament'.

In the evening, as anti-prorogation demonstrators gather in Parliament Square and Whitehall, it emerges that anti-Brexit campaigner Gina Miller has already issued legal proceedings to challenge the decision. Miss Miller tells BBC News that the Prime Minister was 'hijacking the Queen's prerogative power' and using it for 'unscrupulous means'. Former Conservative Prime Minister Sir John Major also says that he is seeking advice on the legality of Mr Johnson's actions.

The fallout from yesterday continues, with Jeremy Corbyn stating, 'what we are going to do is try to politically stop him on Tuesday with a parliamentary process in order to legislate to prevent a no deal Brexit and also to try and prevent him shutting down Parliament in this utterly crucial period'. His comments come in reply to Jacob Rees-Mogg, who travelled to Balmoral yesterday to obtain the Queen's assent to the dissolution of Parliament, telling BBC News, 'all these people who are wailing and gnashing of teeth know that there are two ways of doing what they want to do. One, is to change the government and the other is to change the law. If they do either of those that will then have an effect. If they don't have either the courage or the gumption to do either of those then we will leave on the 31st of October in accordance with the referendum result'.

Ruth Davidson, the Scottish Conservative leader, announces that she will resign, admitting that her political career had taken a toll on her personal life. In her resignation letter she neither criticises nor praises the Prime Minister, saying only that she has 'not hidden the conflict I have felt over Brexit'. Lord Young, a government whip, also resigns saying he was 'very unhappy at the timing and length of the prorogation'.

Momentum's National Coordinator, Laura Parker, announces plans for the group to 'bring the streets of the UK to a standstill' in protest against Boris Johnson's decision to suspend Parliament. The demonstrations are planned for Saturday. At a rally in London the Shadow Chancellor, John McDonnell, denounces the Prime Minister's decision to prorogue Parliament, saying that the British people 'have stood up to dictators before and they will stand up to this one as well'.

Sonia Khan, the media advisor to the Chancellor of the Exchequer, is summarily dismissed by the PM's senior advisor, Dominic Cummings, and escorted out of Downing Street by armed police, after being accused of staying in touch with people close to her former boss, Philip Hammond.

In a series of broadcast interviews, Boris Johnson insists that efforts by MPs to block no deal made the EU less likely to compromise on the Withdrawal Agreement. Speaking to Sky News, the Prime Minister says that MPs had already spent three years debating Brexit 'without actually getting it over the line', adding, 'I am afraid that the more our friends and partners think at the back of their minds that Brexit could be stopped, that the UK could be kept in by Parliament, the less likely they are to give us the deal that we need'.

Former Conservative cabinet minister, Oliver Letwin, insists there is still time to pass legislation that could force the Prime Minister to delay the Brexit date, even if Parliament is prorogued for more than a month from the middle of September. Sir Oliver adds that he hoped that by the end of next week Boris Johnson will know that he must seek an extension and confirms that he has been discussing the options with Commons Speaker John Bercow.

Irish Deputy Prime Minister, Simon Coveney, tells reporters in Helsinki that 'at the moment nothing credible has come from the British Government in the context of an alternative to the backstop. If that changes, great, we will look at it in Dublin, but more importantly it can be the basis of a discussion in Brussels. But it has got to be credible. It can't simply be this notion that "look, we must have the backstop removed and we will solve this problem in the future negotiation" without any credible way of doing that. That's not going to fly and it's important that we are all honest about that'.

Former Prime Minister, Sir John Major, says that he is joining a judicial review being brought by Gina Miller to prevent the suspension of Parliament, saying that it was not acceptable for Boris Johnson to prevent MPs from 'opposing Brexit plans'. Labour's deputy leader, Tom Watson, also declares that he is taking part in the action.

Foreign Secretary Dominic Raab insists that only four days of Commons sitting time would be lost in addition to the already planned party conference break. Speaking to reporters at a meeting of EU foreign ministers in Helsinki he says, 'the idea this is some kind of constitutional outrage is nonsense. It's actually lawful, it's perfectly proper, there is precedent for it and actually, fundamentally, for the people watching this, they want to see that we are leaving the EU but also talking about all the other things they expect us to be addressing'.

A court in Edinburgh refuses to grant an interim injunction blocking the Prime Minister from proroguing the House of Commons before the legal case is heard in full next week. Ruling against the injunction, Judge Lord Doherty says, 'I'm not satisfied that it has been demonstrated that there's a need for an interim suspension or an interim interdict to be granted at this stage'. He does, however, bring the case forward, to be heard next Tuesday, saying, 'it's in the interest of justice that it proceeds sooner rather than later'.

Jeremy Corbyn tweets, 'The public outrage at Boris Johnson shutting down democracy has been deafening. People are right to take to the streets — and I encourage everyone to join the demonstrations in London and across the country tomorrow.' Momentum national organiser Michael Chessum says the organisation is 'encouraging civil disobedience, in whatever form that takes'.

Former Prime Minister, Gordon Brown, speaking in Edinburgh, suggests that European leaders are preparing to scrap the Brexit deadline. 'I believe that next week the European Union will withdraw the October 31st deadline and remove the excuse that Boris Johnson has and the claim that he's making that it's the EU that is being inflexible', he says.

On a day of demonstrations in cities across the UK, Remainers take to the streets to protest against the prorogation of Parliament. In Glasgow, Jeremy Corbyn tells those assembled, 'we're not having it' and that the Government should 'stand aside'. In London, shadow Home Secretary Diane Abbott says, 'we cannot allow Boris Johnson to shut down Parliament' whilst John McDonnell tells the same crowd 'we know what Boris Johnson is up to, it is not very subtle is it?'

Playing down reports of a rift with the Prime Minister following the sacking of his adviser, Sonia Khan, the Chancellor of the Exchequer, Sajid Javid, tells the BBC, 'the relationship is fantastic with the Prime Minister. Before he was Prime Minister, he is someone I got on with incredibly well. It's a real privilege to work with him', adding, 'I'm not going to discuss any personnel issues, it wouldn't be appropriate'.

Former Brexit Secretary, David Davies, demands an end to the Speaker's privilege if he stands for re-election as an MP, calling on Conservative Party Chairman, James Cleverly, to intervene with the Buckingham Conservative Association to get them to field an official Tory candidate. Davies says, 'the reality is now that the gloves are off. Remain supporting MPs, including Mr Bercow, are using every trick in the book and tearing up all precedence to try to prevent the democratic voice of the public from being heard on Brexit. We have to fight this battle in the same way. If that means breaking the precedent of not standing against the Speaker in his constituency at the next General Election, then so be it'.

Sunday 1st September 2019

60 days to Brexit

Writing in the 'Mail On Sunday', Jacob Rees-Mogg describes the outrage over the Government's decision to prorogue Parliament as 'just another conflict between Remainers, still trying to prevent the referendum from being obeyed properly, and a Government pledged to leave the EU, as instructed by the voters three years ago'. The Leader of the House of Commons goes on to say that 'the nation should not be distracted by overblown caricatures and hysterical language, but continue to steer a steady course towards its democratic objective'.

In an article for the 'Sunday Telegraph', the EU's chief Brexit negotiator, Michel Barnier, warns that the backstop was the 'maximum flexibility' which could be offered to a non-member country. He goes on to say, 'I am not optimistic about avoiding a no deal scenario but I remain determined to explore all avenues that the UK government will present that are compatible with the Withdrawal Agreement'.

Shadow Chancellor John McDonnell tells Sky News it would be 'very difficult' to outlaw no deal in the few days of parliamentary time available. Asked if Labour could still push for a confidence vote, he says, 'our view is, we have to use every mechanism we possibly can to prevent a no deal and that clearly is still on the table'.

Reports that the Government intends to treat any bid to extend Brexit and prevent a no deal exit as a confidence issue, with supporting Tory MPs stopped from standing for the party at any forthcoming General Election, draw a harsh response from Philip Hammond. The former chancellor tweets, 'If true, this would be staggeringly hypocritical: 8 members of the current cabinet have defied the party whip this year.'

When asked if the Prime Minister will obey any law that the Commons may pass to prevent a no deal Brexit, Michael Gove tells the BBC, 'Let's see what the legislation says. You're asking me about a pig in a poke. And I will wait to see what legislation the opposition may try to bring forward'. In response, Sir Kier Starmer, the shadow Brexit Secretary, tweets, 'For ministers not to confirm that this Government will accept and comply with legislation lawfully passed is breathtaking. The Prime Minister must make a statement on this straightaway. No Government is above the law.'

Ahead of the reconvening of Parliament tomorrow, following the summer recess, former Prime Minister Tony Blair says in speech in London that the 'right way' to consult the public on Brexit is through a second referendum, not a General Election. 'The Brexiteers are laying a trap, to seem as if pushed into an election against their will, when they're actively preparing for it', he says, adding, 'Jeremy Corbyn should see an election for the elephant trap it is. If the Government tries to force an election, Labour should vote against it'.

The Prime Minister urges Conservative MPs not to join forces with opposition parties to seek an extension to Article 50 and further delay Brexit. Speaking outside Downing Street, he says that, 'if they do, they will plainly chop the legs out from under the UK position and make any negotiation absolutely impossible'. Boris Johnson goes on to say, 'I want everybody to know there are no circumstances in which I will ask Brussels to delay. We are leaving on the 31st of October. No ifs or buts', before adding, 'let our negotiators get on with their work without that sword of Damocles over their necks and without an election, without an election.'

A Government spokesman confirms that any Conservative MPs who vote with the opposition will face the removal of the party whip and expulsion from the parliamentary party. Works and Pensions Secretary, Amber Rudd, warns against such a move, telling 'The Spectator' magazine, 'I'm really urging the Government to think very carefully about taking such a dramatic step. I have made my views clear to the Prime Minister that we should not be a party that is trying to remove from our party two former chancellors, a number of ex-Cabinet ministers – that the way to hold our party together and to get a deal is to bring them onside'. Several Conservative MPs express their intention to vote against the Government, one of them, former International Development Secretary Rory Stewart, telling Sky News, 'I'm a proud Conservative, I support the Conservative Party. I just think a no deal Brexit would be a huge mistake and I have to stop it happening'.

Remain backing MPs release details of the Bill that they will table in the Commons should they succeed in their efforts to take control of the parliamentary timetable. The European Union (Withdrawal) (No 6) Bill will be presented by Labour's Hilary Benn and will require the Government to either reach a deal with the EU or gain Parliament's approval for a no deal exit by October 19th. Mr Benn says, 'if neither of these two conditions have been met, however, by October 19th, the day after the European Council meeting concludes, then the Prime Minister must send a letter to the president of the European Council requesting an Article 50 extension until January 31, 2020'. He goes on to add that, 'if the European Council agrees to an extension to January 31, 2020, then the Prime Minister must immediately accept that extension. If the European Council proposes an extension to a different date, then the Prime Minister must accept that extension within two days, unless the House of Commons rejects it'. Senior government sources confirm that the Prime Minister would table a motion to schedule a General Election for October 15th if MPs pass the Bill.

Tuesday 3rd September 2019

58 days to Brexit

During a court case in Edinburgh, brought by group of 75 MPs and peers to challenge Boris Johnson's decision to prorogue Parliament, it is revealed that the Prime Minister and his most senior aides were discussing the plan almost three weeks ago. A note seen by Boris Johnson and his senior adviser Dominic Cummings, dated August 15th, asked whether the PM wanted to consider prorogation. The word 'yes' was written on the document, and the Prime Minister later replied to the note by saying suspending Parliament should not be 'shocking'.

Parliament returns after the summer recess and, as the Prime Minister addresses the Commons, Conservative MP Phillip Lee crosses the house to sit with the Liberal Democrats, his defection effectively wiping out the Conservative's majority. During his speech, the Prime Minister asserts that there will be 'no further pointless delay' to Brexit, adding, 'enough is enough. The country wants this done and they want the referendum respected'. Ahead of the resumption of Parliament, former ministers Justine Greening and Alistair Burt announce that they will not stand again as Tory candidates.

The Speaker, John Bercow, permits a motion to allow an alliance of Tory and Opposition MPs to attempt to seize control of the Commons' order paper to prevent a no deal Brexit. Mocking the Prime Minister as he does so, the Speaker declares, 'I've done it, I am doing it, I will continue to do it to the best of my ability without fear or favour - to coin a phrase, come what may, do or die'. The motion is passed by 328 votes to 321, with 21 Conservative MPs voting against the Government.

Speaking in the Commons immediately after being defeated in his first vote, Boris Johnson declares that Parliament was 'on the brink of wrecking' the Brexit negotiations. 'The people are going to have to choose', he says before adding, 'I can confirm tonight we are tabling a motion under the Fixed Term Parliaments Act'. A vote in the Commons on whether to hold a General Election is expected tomorrow, with a two thirds majority needed for it to pass. Jeremy Corbyn indicates that his party will only vote for a General Election once the Bill to prevent a no deal Brexit is passed in to law.

Following his defection to the Liberal Democrats, Dr Phillip Lee tells Sky News, 'I guess the elevation of Boris Johnson to the Prime Minister's position has accelerated events. I don't think that everybody who's currently siting as a Conservative is going to be sitting as a Conservative after the next election. Whether they join the Liberal Democrats or not, it's an individual decision but I really wouldn't be surprised if more come to this conclusion over the next few days.'

Late in the evening, a Government spokesman confirms that 'the Chief Whip is speaking with those Tory MPs who did not vote with the Government this evening. They will have the whip removed'. The 21 Tory rebels include eight former ministers and two former Chancellors of the Exchequer.

Shadow Brexit Secretary, Sir Kier Starmer, declares that the Labour Party will not support the Prime Minister in his attempts to call a General Election for October 15th. Speaking to the BBC, Sir Kier says, 'we are not voting for a General Election today. We are not dancing to Boris Johnson's tune. If Johnson says the election will be on 15th October no one trusts him'.

The Government wins the case being heard at the Court of Session in Edinburgh, the court ruling that the Prime Minister's planned suspension of Parliament is lawful and can go ahead. Lord Doherty rules this morning, 'In my view the advice given in relation to the prorogation decision is a matter involving high policy and political judgement. This is political territory and decision-making, which cannot be measured by legal standards but only by political judgments. Accountability for the advice is to Parliament and ultimately the electorate and not to the courts.' Two further legal challenges, one in the High Court in London and another in a court in Belfast, are yet to be heard.

In his first Prime Ministers Questions, Boris Johnson replies to a question from Jeremy Corbyn about food prices by saying 'he is worried about free trade deals with America, but I can see only one chlorinated chicken in the House, and he is sitting on the opposition front bench', ending his exchange with the Labour leader by saying, 'we think that the friends of this country are to be found in Paris, in Berlin and in the White House. He thinks that they are in the Kremlin, in Tehran and in Caracas'.

Following the Chancellor of the Exchequer's spending and investment plans for the 2020/2021 financial year, the House moves on to debate The European Union (Withdrawal) (No 6) Bill which the Prime Minister describes as a 'surrender' Bill, designed to 'overturn the biggest democratic vote in our history' which could delay Brexit 'for many years to come'. Compelling the Prime Minister to seek an extension to Article 50 if no deal is imminent, the Bill passes at second reading by 329 to 300 votes and later at third reading by 327 votes to 299. Later in the evening, the Government negotiates with the opposition and agrees to the Bill completing all of its stages in the House of Lords by Friday, with it returning to the Commons for any further consideration on Monday.

During the debate on the Government's proposed motion under the Fixed Term Parliament Act, calling for a General Election on October 15th, Kenneth Clarke, having had the Tory whip removed yesterday, tells the Commons, 'I do think the Prime Minister, with the greatest respect, has a tremendous skill in keeping a straight face whilst he is being so disingenuous'. The former Chancellor goes on to add, 'it is wrong to say that the opposition to him is trying to reverse the referendum. A very large percentage of those who have been defeating him in the last two days are prepared to vote for Brexit, they have voted for Brexit more often than he has'. The Government win the vote but, with the Labour Party, in the main, abstaining, fall well short of the two thirds majority needed to trigger a General Election. After the vote, Boris Johnson says of Jeremy Corbyn, who was not present in the House for the result, 'I think he has become the first leader of the opposition in the democratic history of our country to refuse the invitation to an election', adding, 'the obvious conclusion is, I'm afraid, that he does not think he will win'.

Speaking at a business event, Ireland's Deputy Prime Minister, Simon Coveney, suggests that, in the event of a no deal Brexit, a hard border between the South and the North may not be necessary. On the subject of customs checks he says, 'we recognise the reality that Ireland will have a responsibility to protect its own place in the single market. That will involve some checks. But I can assure you we will try to do that in a way that limits the risk. And we will try and do it away from the border'.

In a round of media interviews this morning, Chancellor of the Exchequer, Sajid Javid, says of the 21 Conservative MPs who have had the whip withdrawn, 'they are not just my colleagues, these are my friends, they are good Conservatives. They have done so much in public service for our country. At the same time, it is right the Prime Minister has the opportunity to take a critical vote and make it a matter of confidence'. Asked if there was a chance of redemption for the rebels, the Chancellor replies, 'I hope so. I would like to see those colleagues come back at some point but right now the Prime Minister had no choice'.

The Prime Minister's brother, Jo Johnson, announces that he is standing down as both Universities Minister and a Conservative MP. In a tweet, Mr Johnson says, 'It's been an honour to represent Orpington for 9 years & to serve as a minister under three PMs. In recent weeks I've been torn between family loyalty and the national interest - it's an unresolvable tension & time for others to take on my roles as MP & Minister.'

Gina Miller's High Court legal challenge to the suspension of Parliament begins in London today with Lord Pannick QC telling the Court, 'our case is that the Prime Minister's advice to Her Majesty to prorogue Parliament for the period of five weeks is an unlawful abuse of power'. The case will be heard by three of the most senior judges in Britain who will initially consider whether the case is justiciable and can proceed before taking evidence from witnesses.

French European Affairs Minister Amelie de Montchalin says that another delay 'would not solve the UK's Brexit 'problem', suggesting that even a six-month extension would not be long enough for Britain to sort out the mess. Her colleague Jean-Yves Le Drian, the country's Foreign Minister, adds that a no deal Brexit on October 31st is still the 'most likely scenario'. Guy Verhofstadt, chair of the Brexit Steering Group, criticises Boris Johnson's description of the anti no deal legislation passed by Parliament as a 'surrender bill'. He says, 'opposing a no deal is not surrender. This is the language of Europe's dark past. It implies Britain's European allies and neighbours are enemies. I refuse to believe the majority of British people think this is the case'.

During a speech to business leaders in Glasgow, the former Prime Minister Sir John Major condemns the decision to withdraw the whip and deselect the 21 rebel Tory MPs who voted to allow Remainers to take over the Parliamentary order paper on Tuesday. He accuses Boris Johnson of running a 'Government by bluster and threat in a climate of aggressive bullying' and turning the Conservatives into a 'mean-minded sect', adding that the current Cabinet was 'a faction of a faction, with no counter-balance of opinion to hold it back'.

In Wakefield, West Yorkshire, during a speech promoting his plans to increase police numbers, the Prime Minister declares that he would 'rather be dead in a ditch' than delay Brexit further. He also adds that he hated 'banging on about Brexit' declaring, 'I don't want an election at all, but frankly I cannot see any other way'. After his speech, it emerges that the Prime Minister, and his girlfriend Carrie Symonds will visit the Queen in Balmoral, a spokesman stressing that it was normal for the Prime Minister to spend a weekend with the monarch at this time of year and that the trip had been in the diary for a long time.

Friday 6th September 2019

55 days to Brexit

The main opposition parties all claim that they will either vote against the government or abstain if the Prime Minister makes another attempt at the start of next week to go to the country on October 15th. A Liberal Democrat spokesperson says, 'we were all clear we are not going to let Boris Johnson cut and run. The Liberal Democrat position for a while now is that we won't vote for a General Election until we have an extension agreed with the EU. I think the others are coming around to that. As a group we will all vote against or abstain on Monday'. Emily Thornberry, the shadow Foreign Secretary, tells the BBC that Labour need to be 'absolutely sure' that the UK will not leave the EU without a deal before agreeing to an election, adding that the 'immediate crisis in front of us has to be sorted before we do anything else'.

The Prime Minister hints that there could be a path back to the Conservative Party for the 21 rebels he stripped of the whip this week after they voted to block no deal. Speaking in Scotland, he tells reporters, 'yes of course I'm going to reach out to those colleagues and have been reaching out to them to try and find ways of building bridges but I've got to be clear we must get Brexit done and that's my message to my colleagues'.

Pro-EU campaigner Gina Miller loses her legal bid to prevent the prorogation of Parliament. Rejecting Mrs Miller's case, the Lord Chief Justice, Lord Burnett, says, 'we have concluded that, whilst we should grant permission to apply for judicial review, the claim must be dismissed'. Outside court, Mrs Miller says she was 'very disappointed with the judgment', but vows to take the case to the Supreme Court later this month.

Boris Johnson writes to all Tory members indicating that he would rather defy the law than beg Brussels for a delay in taking the UK out of the EU. The Prime Minister says he is only bound 'in theory' by The European Union (Withdrawal) (No 6) Bill, commonly referred to as the Benn Act, a law which is expected to receive Royal Assent on Monday and effectively take a no deal Brexit off the table. In his letter, he reiterates his determination to stand firm saying, 'they just passed a law that would force me to beg Brussels for an extension to the Brexit deadline. This is something I will never do'.

At a meeting of political aides, the Prime Minister's senior adviser, Dominic Cummings, says, 'we will not be going to Brussels and asking for an extension. MPs will have one more chance on Monday to do the right thing or we are going to send them home that evening and they can spend the next four weeks taking us to court and complaining. It will then be us going to the European Council next month and we will not be asking for an extension'.

In an article in the 'Daily Telegraph', the former Conservative Party leader, Iain Duncan Smith, suggests that Boris Johnson would be 'martyred' if he chooses to break the law and risk a possible prison sentence for contempt of Parliament. He goes on to say, 'this is about Parliament versus the people. Boris Johnson is on the side of the people, who voted to leave the EU. The people are sovereign because they elect Parliament. But Parliament wants to stop the will of the people'. Priti Patel, the Home Secretary, tells 'The Telegraph' that Jeremy Corbyn was showing 'disdain for democracy' and causing 'bewilderment and anger' among voters, accusing him of blocking a General Election because he thinks the public 'can't be trusted to decide'. Thirsk and Malton MP Kevin Hollinrake tweets, 'any media speculation about Govt ignoring legislation is nonsense. Even if it was under consideration, which I'm sure it's not, you would see a very significant number of Conservative MPs resigning the whip, including myself'.

Sir Nicholas Soames, one of the 21 Tory rebels expelled from the Conservative Party, tells 'The Times' that the current Prime Minister is nothing like his grandfather, saying, 'Boris Johnson is nothing like Winston Churchill. I don't think anyone has called Boris a diplomat or statesman'. He goes on to add that the Prime Minister is 'deeply unreliable' and is someone who 'doesn't like the House of Commons'.

Amber Rudd, the Work and Pensions Secretary, resigns from the Cabinet and the Conservative Party, announcing that she would be standing as an independent Conservative in her Hastings and Rye constituency at the next General Election. In her resignation letter, Ms Rudd says that she no longer believes 'leaving with a deal is the Government's main objective'. She also goes on to say, 'I must also address the assault on decency and democracy that took place last week when you sacked 21 loyal One Nation Conservatives. This short-sighted culling of my colleagues has stripped the Party of broadminded and dedicated Conservative MPs. I cannot support this act of political vandalism'.

The Government announces this morning that Therese Coffey, an environment minister, has replaced Amber Rudd as Work and Pensions Secretary.

Dominic Raab, the Foreign Secretary, defends the decision to sack 21 rebel MPs, telling Sky News that the Prime Minister was 'right to restore some discipline'. He also says, of Amber Rudd's resignation, 'in fairness, when she took the Cabinet role everyone was asked do you accept and will you sign up to and do you support the Prime Minister's plan to leave by October, preferably with a deal but if not come what may? We all accepted that and I think that the Prime Minister was right to restore some discipline and I think he is right to expect it from his top team'. Mr Raab also goes on to say that the government will 'test to the limit' the anti no deal legislation passed in the Commons last week.

In a series of newspaper advertisements, the Brexit Party offer to prop up Boris Johnson in Downing Street as long as he commits to leaving the EU without a deal. The advert, featuring Nigel Farage and the Prime Minister standing face to face, says, 'Let's have a clean-break Brexit, then we will help you secure a big Brexit majority and destroy Corbyn's Labour. Together we would be unstoppable.' Mr Farage tells 'The Sunday Times' that he is ready to offer a 'non-aggression pact' to the Prime Minister that he predicts could win a 100 seat majority for the Tories and Brexit Party. A survey for 'The Sunday Times' finds that seven in 10 people who vote Conservative and eight in 10 Brexit Party backers are in favour of an electoral pact before the next General Election.

Business Secretary Andrea Leadsom confirms that the Conservative Party will defy convention and put up a candidate against the Commons Speaker in the next General Election. Writing in the 'Mail on Sunday' Ms Leadsom says that, by allowing MPs to take over the parliamentary timetable, the Speaker 'hasn't just bent the rules, he has broken them'. The Business Secretary goes on to describe Mr Bercow's decision to allow last Tuesday's vote to take over the Commons order paper as 'a flagrant abuse', adding, 'it is right that the Conservatives will recognise this fact at the next General Election by standing our candidate in Buckingham'.

John McDonnell tells Andrew Marr on the BBC that any caretaker Prime Minister must be Jeremy Corbyn because 'he is the leader of the Opposition'. The Shadow Chancellor adds, of the House of Commons, 'just as he has united them over these last few weeks, he could do that as caretaker Prime Minister. I think we could unite them under Jeremy Corbyn'.

Jean-Yves Le Drian, the French Foreign Minister, says the Brexit situation in the UK is 'very worrying' and suggests that an extension would not be possible under the current circumstances. 'We are not going to do this every three months', he says. His comments are echoed by Guy Verhofstadt, who tweets, 'Foreign Minister Le Drian is right: yet another extension for Brexit is unacceptable unless the deadlock in London is broken. Let it be a 2nd ref, new elections, a revocation of art 50 or the approval of the deal, but not today's hopeless status quo.'

The Conservative Party opens up a 14 point lead over Labour in a new YouGov survey, with Labour trailing on 21 percent, the Lib Dems on 19 percent and the Brexit Party on 12 percent.

Speaking ahead of his first meeting with Boris Johnson in Dublin tomorrow, the Irish Prime Minister, Leo Varadkar, indicates that he does not expect a breakthrough. 'I don't think the meeting tomorrow is a high stakes meeting, as I don't anticipate a big breakthrough tomorrow. If we come to an agreement that agreement will happen in October at the EU summit', he says. Mr Varadkar goes on to add, 'it will be an opportunity to get to know each other a little bit better, to see if there is common ground. I'm sure there will be'.

Responding to suggestions that the Government plans to send a letter to the EU requesting an extension to Article 50, as the law that passed on to the statute books today requires, and then send another asking the EU to ignore it, former Supreme Court justice Lord Sumption tells BBC Radio 4's 'Today' programme that 'to send the letter and then try to neutralise it seems to me, plainly, a breach of the Act'. Conservative MP Andrew Bridgen tells the 'Daily Mail' that becoming a 'martyr to democracy' could be Boris Johnson's only option. 'Unfortunately, democracy has an insatiable appetite for martyrs', Mr Bridgen says, adding, 'he could end up being one of those - collateral damage'.

Downing Street confirms that prorogation of Parliament will happen this evening even if the Prime Minister loses his latest effort to force a snap election.

Boris Johnson and Leo Varadkar meet in Dublin but with little sign of any progress being made. At a joint press conference afterwards the Prime Minister says, 'I want to find a deal. I have looked carefully at no deal. Yes, we could do it, the UK could certainly get through it, but be in no doubt that outcome would be a failure of statecraft for which we would all be responsible. I would overwhelmingly prefer to find an agreement. I do believe that a deal can be done by October 18th so let's do it together'. Mr Varadkar warns that the UK has no 'realistic' plan for replacing the insurance policy for the Irish border. 'No backstop is no deal', he says.

Former Scottish Tory leader, Ruth Davidson, criticises the decision to remove the whip from 21 Tory MPs saying that they 'weren't serial rebels'. 'Kicking 21 Conservatives, many very senior and well known by the public, out of the party makes us less of a broad church and, in voters' minds, less representative of the country as a whole', she writes in the 'Evening Standard', adding, 'as satisfying as it might have been for those in Number 10 frustrated by the Commons stalling on Brexit, it may still prove as "short-sighted" as Amber Rudd predicts'.

The Speaker of the House of Commons, John Bercow, announces his intention to resign from his post by the end of October. In a statement to the House Mr Bercow says, 'at the 2017 election, I promised my wife and children that it would be my last. This is a pledge that I intend to keep. If the House votes tonight for an early General Election, my tenure as Speaker and MP will end when this Parliament ends. If the House does not so vote, I have concluded that the least disruptive and most democratic course of action would be for me to stand down at the close of business on Thursday, October 31st.'

Dominic Grieve, the former Conservative Attorney General, leads a Humble Address in the House of Commons designed to compel Downing Street advisers to give MPs their WhatsApp, Facebook and text messages, as well as personal emails relating to the prorogation of Parliament. The address also calls for the release of the document 'Operation Yellowhammer' which is said to detail the potential threats from a no deal Brexit, giving a deadline of 11pm on the 11th September for the Government to comply. He wins the vote by 311 to 302, but the Government indicates they will not comply with the order to release personal communications, with Geoffrey Cox, the current Attorney General, saying the move risks a 'trespass on fundamental rights of individuals' and Michael Gove claiming the move will 'trample over data protection law, ECHR rights and the principle of safe space'.

Parliament's final task before prorogation is the Government's second attempt to call an early General Election under the Fixed Term Parliament Act. Opening the debate, the Prime Minister says that the opposition parties 'have been trying to disguise their preposterous yellow bellies by coming up with ever more outrageous excuses for delaying an election until the end of October, or perhaps November, or perhaps until hell freezes over'. In reply, Jeremy Corbyn accuses the Prime Minister of 'running away' by proroguing Parliament until October 14th. The Government achieve only 293 of the 434 votes needed to pass the motion, 5 fewer than they received in a similar vote last week. Speaking after the vote, the Prime Minister says, 'no matter how many devices this Parliament invents to tie my hands I will try to get an agreement in the national interest', adding, 'this Government will not allow Brexit to be delayed any further'.

Tuesday 10th September 2019

51 days to Brexit

The EU's new trade commissioner, Phil Hogan, stokes speculation that the Prime Minister is exploring moves that could leave Northern Ireland closely aligned to the EU whilst the rest of the UK makes a clean break. Mr Hogan claims that 'the penny is finally dropping', saying, 'Johnson has made a proposal talking about an all-Ireland food zone. That is certainly a clear indication of divergence between Northern Ireland and the Republic of Ireland, the EU and the rest of the UK. If we can build on that, we certainly might get closer to one another in terms of a possible outcome'. DUP leader Arlene Foster, however, pours cold water on the idea. After talks with Boris Johnson in Number 10 she says the Prime Minister had 'confirmed his rejection of a Northern Ireland-only backstop', adding that any deal that did not have the support of both communities in the Province was 'doomed to failure'.

On a visit to a school in London, Boris Johnson rejects criticism that his decision to suspend Parliament for five weeks was undemocratic. 'What a load of nonsense', the Prime Minister is reported as saying, adding, 'we were very, very clear that if people wanted a democratic moment, if they wanted an election, we offered it to the Labour opposition, and mysteriously they decided not to go for it'.

Last week's decision by the Court of Session in Edinburgh that the prorogation of Parliament is legal is overturned by a panel of three judges on appeal. Their judgement says, 'The Inner House of the Court of Session has ruled that the Prime Minister's advice to HM the Queen that the United Kingdom Parliament should be prorogued from a day between 9th and 12th September until 14th October was unlawful because it had the purpose of stymying Parliament.' The judgement goes on to say, 'the court will accordingly make an order declaring that the Prime Minister's advice to HM the Queen and the prorogation which followed thereon was unlawful and is thus null and of no effect'. A Government spokesman responds by saying, 'we are disappointed by today's decision, and will appeal to the UK Supreme Court. The UK Government needs to bring forward a strong domestic legislative agenda. Proroguing Parliament is the legal and necessary way of delivering this'.

The High Court in London reveals that it views the situation completely differently from the Scottish judges. Following last Friday's decision to dismiss the case brought by Gina Miller, and supported by Sir John Major, a bench led by Lord Chief Justice Lord Burnett deliver their ruling at a brief hearing in London today. The judgement says, 'we concluded that the decision of the Prime Minister was not justiciable (capable of challenge). It is not a matter for the courts.' It goes on to conclude that, 'the Prime Minister's decision that Parliament should be prorogued at the time and for the duration chosen and the advice given to Her Majesty to do so in the present case were political. They were inherently political in nature and there are no legal standards against which to judge their legitimacy'.

Speaking in his second Facebook PMQ's, Boris Johnson says, 'if opposition members of Parliament disagree with our approach, then it is always open to them to take up the offer I made twice now, twice, that we should have an election', adding, 'there is nothing more democratic in this country than a General Election. We will get on and we will come out of the EU on October 31st'.

The Labour Party Deputy Leader says that the 2016 referendum was too long ago to now be valid, and that a single-issue election would not break the Brexit deadlock. Speaking in London, Tom Watson claims that, 'the only way to break the Brexit deadlock once and for all is a public vote in a referendum'. He goes on to say, 'very difficult though it was, I and many others respected the result of the 2016 referendum for a long time', but adds, 'there eventually comes a point, and we are very far past it now, when circumstances are so changed that a years-old plebiscite is no longer a valid basis on which to take such a momentous decision about the future of the UK'. Conservative Party Chairman, James Cleverly, responds by saying, 'Labour's deputy leader makes it clear Labour want to cancel the referendum result. This latest trick would mean delaying Brexit again for up to a year, handing over £250million a week to Brussels for no purpose'.

In a speech that appears to contradict his deputy leader, Sir Kier Starmer tell the Trades Union Congress in Brighton that a General Election must come before any referendum. The shadow Brexit

Secretary says, 'Brexit will of course be a crucial issue at this election', adding Jeremy Corbyn was right to say 'that an incoming Labour government will commit to a referendum'. Sir Kier goes on to confirm that 'remain should and will be on the ballot paper along with a credible option to leave'.

The 'Operation Yellowhammer' document is published, in compliance with Dominic Grieve's successful motion in the Commons on Monday. The document, described by Michael Gove as a 'reasonable worst case scenario', warns of delays at port crossings, saying, 'the lack of trader readiness combined with limited space in French ports to hold unready HGVs could reduce the flow rate to 40-60 per cent of current levels within one day as unready HGVs will fill the ports and block flow', the result being that, 'HGVs could face maximum delays of 1.5-2.5 days before being able to cross the border'. Citizens travelling to and from the EU will face increased immigration checks, the report says, 'dependent on the plans EU member states put in place to cope with these increased immigration checks, it is likely that delays will occur for UK arrivals and departures at EU airports and ports'.

Addressing the subject of energy supply, the 'Operation Yellowhammer' document suggests that 'demand for energy will be met and there will be no disruption to electricity or gas interconnections', but warns, 'there will likely be significant electricity price increases for consumers'. Warning of medicine shortages, the document goes on to outline that, 'the reliance of medicines and medicinal products' supply chains on the short straits crossing make them particularly vulnerable to severe extended delays', adding that, 'while some products can be stockpiled, others cannot due to short shelf lives.' The report says that although there will not be an overall shortage of food in the UK, 'critical dependencies for the food supply chain (such as key ingredients, chemicals and packaging) may be in shorter supply' which will 'reduce availability and choice of products and increase price'.

On the subject of Gibraltar, the 'Yellowhammer' dossier says that 'prolonged border delays over the longer term are likely to adversely impact Gibraltar's economy', the report expressing concern that 'Gibraltar has still not taken decisions to invest in contingency infrastructure' or 'passed all necessary legislation for no deal'. On fishing, 'Yellowhammer' says that vessels fishing illegally in UK waters 'is likely to cause anger and frustration in the UK catching sector, which could lead to both clashes between fishing vessels and an increase in non-compliance in the domestic fleet' which would, along with an increase in border violations, 'put enforcement and response capabilities at risk'. On social care, the dossier says, 'there is an assumption that there will be no major change in adult social care on the day after EU exit', but warns that 'an increase in inflation following EU exit would significantly impact adult social care providers due to increasing staff and supply costs, and may lead to provider failure'.

Responding to the release of 'Operation Yellowhammer', shadow Brexit Secretary Sir Keir Starmer says, 'these documents confirm the severe risks of a no deal Brexit, which Labour has worked so hard to block. It is completely irresponsible for the Government to have tried to ignore these stark warnings and prevent the public from seeing the evidence. Boris Johnson must now admit that he has been dishonest with the British people about the consequence of a no deal Brexit. It is also now more important than ever that Parliament is recalled and has the opportunity to scrutinise these documents and take all steps necessary to stop no deal'. Speaking on ITV's 'Peston', Nigel Farage dismisses fears of food shortages as 'complete and utter rubbish'. The Brexit Party leader says, 'I've never seen such utter tosh in my entire life, unlike these civil servants sitting in Whitehall I spent 20 years in international trade, buying and selling goods, and shipping them all over the world. The idea given that there are over 100 active ports in the United Kingdom, that even if there was a problem at Dover there would be food shortages, is complete and utter rubbish. It's Project Fear Mark II, and it should be utterly, totally, completely disregarded'.

Thursday 12th September 2019

49 days to Brexit

The High Court in Belfast rules that the Government's approach to Brexit does not breach the Good Friday Agreement. Lord Justice Bernard McCloskey gives his decision in Belfast on three joined cases, including the argument that no deal on October 31st would undermine agreements involving the UK and Irish governments that were struck during the peace process. Dismissing calls for the courts to step in, the judge says that the issues at stake are 'inherently and unmistakeably political'.

Speaking in London the Prime Minister, when asked if he lied to the Queen, replies 'absolutely not', adding, 'the High Court in England plainly agrees with us but the Supreme Court will have to decide'. Boris Johnson goes on to say, 'the British judiciary, the United Kingdom judiciary, is one of the great glories of our constitution - they are independent. Believe me, around the world people look at our judges with awe and admiration, so I'm not going to quarrel or criticise the judges'.

Jean-Claude Juncker, the EU President, tells the Euronews channel, 'the British were told for more than 40 years that they were in but they didn't want to share all the policies that have been decided. The British from the very beginning were part-time Europeans, what we need is full-time Europeans'. Elsewhere in Europe, Michel Barnier, the EU's chief negotiator, says that he is ready to look at 'any concrete legally operational proposals from the UK' on how to break the current backstop deadlock. Their comments come as Boris Johnson declares that he is 'very hopeful' of a deal. 'I think we can see the rough area of a landing space, of how you can do it - it will be tough, it will be hard, but I think we can get there', the Prime Minister says, adding, 'but if we have to come out without a deal on October 31st, we will be ready'.

At a lecture in London, the out-going Commons Speaker, John Bercow, warns the Prime Minister not to ignore the law that requires him to seek an extension to Article 50 if no Brexit deal is forthcoming. 'If that demands additional procedural creativity in order to come to pass', the Speaker says, 'it is a racing certainty that this will happen and that neither the limitations of the existing rulebook nor the ticking of the clock will stop it doing so'. The Speaker goes on to say, 'let me make myself crystal clear, ladies and gentlemen, the only form of Brexit which we will have, whenever that might be, will be a Brexit that the House of Commons has explicitly endorsed'.

Friday 13th September 2019

48 days to Brexit

In an interview with 'The Times' ahead of the release of his memoirs, David Cameron says he is 'truly sorry' for the uncertainty caused by the referendum he called, saying he has 'many regrets' about the vote and how he 'failed'. The former Prime Minister goes on to add, 'I did not fully anticipate the strength of feeling that would be unleashed both during the referendum and afterwards, and I am truly sorry to have seen the country I love so much suffer uncertainty and division in the years since then', but goes on to say that putting membership of the European Union to a public vote was 'not just fair and overdue, but inevitable'. Mr Cameron also criticises Boris Johnson and Michael Gove over their conduct during the EU referendum, accusing them of acting 'appallingly' and 'trashing the government', adding that they 'left the truth at home' with claims that EU membership cost £350million a week and that Turkey would soon be joining the bloc.

Ahead of planned talks on Monday with Jean-Claude Juncker and Michel Barnier, the Prime Minister says that he is 'cautiously optimistic'. Speaking in Rotherham, Boris Johnson says, 'we are working incredibly hard to get a deal. There is the rough shape of the deal to be done. As some of you may have seen, I myself have been to talk to various other EU leaders, particularly in Germany, in France and in Ireland, where we made a good deal of progress'. His upbeat mood is echoed by Phil Hogan, who will become the EU's lead negotiator on a post-Brexit trade deal. Mr Hogan says, 'recent events in London give us cause for some optimism'.

Responding to suggestions that Government have been examining proposals for customs arrangements that would apply only to Northern Ireland, rather than aligning the whole UK with EU market rules, Arlene Foster, the leader of the DUP, says that the 'UK must leave as one nation', adding, 'we are keen to see a sensible deal but not one that divides the internal market of the UK'. The idea is also played down by the Irish Prime Minister, who tells RTE Radio, 'we have always said we would be willing to look at alternative arrangements but what we're seeing falls far short'.

The Speaker of the House of Commons joins demands for Parliament to be recalled, telling the 'Evening Standard' that 'there are voices to be heard, there are arguments still to be thrashed out'. John Bercow continues, 'surely at a time of a grave public policy challenge on the biggest issue the UK has faced since the Second World War, MPs should for the most part be at their place of work?'

Extracts from his upcoming autobiography, serialised in 'The Times', see David Cameron accusing Boris Johnson of expediency over Brexit. He alleges that the current Prime Minister wanted to be the 'darling of the party' and 'didn't want to risk allowing someone else with a high profile - Michael Gove in particular - to win that crown'. Mr Cameron goes on to say, 'the conclusion I am left with is that he risked an outcome he didn't believe in because it would help his political career'. On Mr Gove himself, the former Prime Minister says, 'one quality shone through: disloyalty. Disloyalty to me and, later, disloyalty to Boris'.

Sam Gymah, one of the 21 rebel Conservative MPs who had the whip withdrawn by Boris Johnson, defects to the Liberal Democrats. Jo Swinson's party's latest recruit was revealed on the first day of their conference in Bournemouth, with Mr Gyimah telling the assembled delegates, 'when people stand up, you're called collaborators. You're called saboteurs. You're called mutineers. Something has gone wrong'. The MP for East Surrey also says that he was 'never what you would call a typical Tory', explaining that he had joined the Lib Dems because liberal values were 'under threat' in his old party.

In an interview with the 'Mail on Sunday' ahead of tomorrow's meeting with Jean-Claude Juncker and Michel Barnier, Boris Johnson says, 'I'm very confident. When I got this job everybody was saying there can be absolutely no change to the Withdrawal Agreement, the backstop was immutable, the arrangements by which the UK was kept locked in to the EU for ever, they said no one could change that', adding, 'they have already moved off that and, as you know, there's a very, very good conversation going on about how to address the issues of the Northern Irish border. A huge amount of progress is being made'. He also warns, 'don't be fooled by Corbyn and the Remain ringleaders. On the one hand they say I don't want a deal. On the other they want to force me to extend. Both are wrong. I am straining to get a deal, but I will also end the uncertainty and take us out on October 31st'. In response, Jean-Claude Juncker tells a German radio station, 'we do not know what the British want in detail, precisely and accurately, and we are still waiting for alternative proposals. Time is running out'.

The Brexit Secretary, Steve Barclay, tells Sky News, 'there has been a huge amount of work going on behind the scenes. We can see a landing zone in terms of a future deal but there is significant work still to do'. Steve Baker, Tory MP and leader of the European Research Group, hints that the groups stance on a deal may be softening saying, of the talks tomorrow, that Boris Johnson should 'prepare for glory'. He also adds, however, that 'if the deal is so bad I have to vote against it, I will not be concerned by the loss of the Conservative whip because the Conservative Party will be in its death throes'.

The ongoing serialisation of David Cameron's memoirs reveals that European President Jean-Claude Juncker promised him that he would 'make Brexit work', but added, 'of course, I've got to say 'No big deal for Britain', but I have to say these things to keep the European Parliament happy'.

Delegates at the Liberal Democrat conference in Bournemouth vote overwhelmingly to support a motion to revoke Article 50 if the party comes to power. Leader Jo Swinson tells the BBC, 'if the Liberal Democrats win a majority at the next election, if people put into government, as a majority government, the "Stop Brexit" party, then stopping Brexit is exactly what people will get. Yes, we will revoke Article 50'. James Cleverly, chairman of the Conservative Party, responds by saying, 'despite calling herself a 'democrat', Jo Swinson's mask has slipped and we now know that she wants to overrule one of the largest democratic votes in British history, cancelling Brexit'.

Boris Johnson and Jean-Claude Juncker meet in Luxembourg. A statement issued by the EU afterwards says that it was the 'UK's responsibility to come forward with legally operational solutions that are compatible with the Withdrawal Agreement', adding, 'such proposals have not yet been made'. The Prime Minister later meets the Prime Minister of Luxembourg, Xavier Bettel, at the Ministry of State building, where he is heckled by a crowd of noisy anti-Brexit protesters. Following their meeting, Boris Johnson declines to take part in a press conference in front of the protesters, requesting it be moved indoors, but Mr Bettel refuses and goes ahead anyway. Gesturing to the empty podium, the Luxembourg Prime Minister says, 'now it's on Mr Johnson, he holds the future of all UK citizens and every EU citizen living in the UK in his hands. It's his responsibility'. Answering questions from reporters on the prospect of a deal, Mr Bettel replies, 'there are no concrete proposals for the moment on the table. And I won't give an agreement to ideas. We need written proposals and the time is ticking'.

Speaking to reporters later, at the UK ambassador's residence, the Prime Minister explains his decision not to take part in the earlier press conference saying, 'I don't think it would've been fair to the Prime Minister of Luxembourg. I think there was clearly going to be a lot of noise and I think our points might've been drowned out'. He goes on to deny the EU claim that he has no legally operational proposals saying, 'papers have been shared but we are now at the stage where we need to start accelerating that work', before adding that he will 'obey the law, but we will come out on October 31st'.

The Liberal Democrats policy of revoking Article 50 should they come to power attracts criticism from within the party, with former health minister Norman Lamb telling BBC Radio 4 that it was a 'threat to the union' and that it risks the Lib Dems being viewed as 'a single-issue party'. Lib Dem peer Lord Paul Scriven also tweets that, 'our new policy on Article 50 is wrong', going on to say, 'we will not help to bring the country together if we unilaterally act in this way'.

It is revealed that Sir John Major will give evidence in the Supreme Court case against Boris Johnson's decision to suspend Parliament. The hearing, which starts tomorrow, will see the former Prime Minister support the claim, brought by Gina Miller, that the five-week prorogation of Parliament breached 'the legal principle of Parliamentary sovereignty' and was thus an 'abuse of power'.

The Supreme Court, with a panel of eleven judges, begins its three-day hearing to reconcile the contradictory judgments issued by the English and Scottish courts regarding the prorogation of Parliament. Opening the proceedings, Gina Miller's barrister, Lord Pannick QC, tells the court, 'the exceptional length of the prorogation in this case is strong evidence that the Prime Minister's motive was to silence Parliament for that period because he sees Parliament as an obstacle to the furtherance of his political aims', adding, 'no Prime Minister has abused his power in the manner in which we allege in at least the last 50 years'. He goes on to stress that he was 'making no criticism of the monarch' in these proceedings, stressing, 'Her Majesty acted on the advice of her Prime Minister', but suggests that the Queen had been misled by the Government and that Boris Johnson's refusal to give evidence to the court should be held against him by the judges.

At the hearing in the Supreme Court, Advocate General for Scotland Lord Keen gives an undertaking that the Prime Minister will comply with the Court's final ruling expected next week, saying, 'if this court finds that the advice of the Prime Minister was unlawful, the Prime Minister will take all necessary steps to comply with any declaration made by the court. The consequence could be that he goes to the Queen and seeks the recall of Parliament'. When asked by Supreme Court justice Lord Kerr 'Would he prorogue Parliament again?', Lord Keen replies, 'I'm not in a position to comment on that. That will have to be addressed by the decision maker'.

During her keynote speech at the Liberal Democrat conference, Jo Swinson says of Boris Johnson, 'Silencing critics. Purging opponents. Ignoring the law. For someone who proclaims to hate socialist dictators, he's doing a pretty good impression of one'. Of the leader of the opposition she says, 'Nigel Farage might be Brexit by name, but it is very clear that Jeremy Corbyn is Brexit by nature'.

Jean-Claude Juncker updates the European Parliament on his meeting with Boris Johnson yesterday, telling the assembly that the lunch had been 'friendly' but he could not 'look you in the eye and tell you progress has been achieved'. To the backdrop of heckling from Brexit Party MEPs, the EU President reiterates that he is ready to work 'day and night' to get an agreement with the UK, but warns that the risk of no deal is 'palpable'. In response, Nigel Farage refers to Xavier Bettel as the 'pipsqueak Prime Minister of Luxembourg who set out to ritually humiliate a British Prime Minister in the most astonishing way, only to greeted as a hero by President Macron at the Elysee Palace'. Mr Farage goes on to say, 'the only way forward now is to deliver on the referendum with a clean break Brexit. Once we have done that, we will have a grown-up conversation about trade and about the way forward'.

In a letter to the 800,000 Poles who currently live in the UK, the Polish ambassador, Arkady Rzegocki, writes, 'I encourage you to seriously consider the possibility of returning to your homeland', adding, 'soon, Great Britain, which has been home to thousands of Poles for generations, will most likely cease to be a member of the European Union, which we regret, but we also see this process as an opportunity to strengthen the bond between our two countries'.

Boris Johnson's QC tells the Supreme Court that his decision to prorogue Parliament was 'fundamentally political' and 'is not territory a court can enter', adding that any suggestion that the Prime Minister's intention was to 'stymy Parliament' is 'untenable'. Opening the Government's case today, Sir James Eadie says that prorogation of Parliament was 'not at all' unusual and added that any application made by Gina Miller's legal team to cross examine the Prime Minister would be 'resisted like fury'.

Northern Ireland's chief constable warns that his officers would be in 'direct threat of attack' if they had to patrol border checkpoints following a hard Brexit. Simon Byrne tells 'The Guardian', 'we are very clear here. We do not support the establishment of checkpoints or monitoring cameras right near the border and we'd be very reluctant to be drawn there because of the threat to our officers'. He goes on to add that, 'history shows us that far more police officers and 20,000 soldiers could not protect the border, so I doubt we are going to do it now'.

In a tweet, Caroline Lucas, leader of the Green Party, condemns the new Liberal Democrat policy which would see Article 50 revoked should the party come to power. She writes, 'Brexit referendum didn't deliver the outcome many of us hoped for, but you can't pretend the result didn't happen. LibDems are doing just that. You can't turn back the clock. Nor ignore the 17m who voted Leave. This doesn't strengthen our democracy. It further imperils it.'

The case at the Supreme Court in to the prorogation of Parliament receives written evidence from Sir John Major. In his statement, the former Prime Minister says, 'it could hardly be suggested that the duties of the Prime Minister to the monarch are less than those of an estate agent to a homeowner. Accordingly, if the court is satisfied that the Prime Minister's decision was materially influenced by something other than the stated justification, that decision must be unlawful'. He goes on to argue that Boris Johnson's justification, that he wanted a new Queen's Speech legislative programme, 'makes no sense and cannot be the true explanation'. The 11 Supreme Court judges are expected to deliver a ruling sometime next week.

A new YouGov opinion poll puts the Liberal Democrats on 23 points, 4 ahead of Labour, with the Conservatives remaining unchanged on 32. In response, former Prime Minister, Tony Blair, tells BBC Radio 4, 'what will destroy the two-party system is if it becomes clear that the two main parties have moved so far away from the centre that the gap in the centre has to be filled in order to be representative of the state of opinion. You only have to look at the Liberal Democrats now, at their party conference. For the first time in a long time, they are looking a much more serious group of people. They have got a coherent argument. If I was the two main parties at the moment, I would worry a lot about that'.

On the day of the publication of his memoirs, former Prime Minister David Cameron tells the BBC, 'I very much hope that Boris Johnson is going to go to Brussels, get a deal, bring it home and take it through Parliament. That is the right thing to do and I wish him well as he tries to do that. I know it is what he wants to do and if he does that I think that will enable him to perhaps reunite the Conservative Party and give back the whip to those that he has taken it away from and the issue can at least get towards some sort of resolution'.

In an interview with Sky News, Jean-Claude Juncker says, 'I don't have an erotic relationship to the backstop. If the results are there, I don't care about it'. Asked if that meant it could be removed, he replies, 'if the objectives are met - all of them - then we don't need the backstop. It was a guarantee, not an aim by itself'.

Shadow Foreign Secretary, Emily Thornberry, says, in a magazine interview, 'the Lib Dems have gotten kind of Taliban, haven't they? They've said they're just going to revoke, there's not going to be another referendum. I don't think it's very democratic to seek to overturn a referendum without asking the people first'. Her comments are addressed swiftly by Jo Swinson who says it was a 'ludicrous' comparison to make, adding, 'Emily is the shadow Foreign Secretary, and should use language that reflects the importance of that role'. Chukka Umunna, a recent defector to the Libs Dems, demands that Ms Thornberry withdraw her 'inappropriate remarks', adding that comparing the party to a 'murderous organisation is no laughing matter'.

Irish deputy Prime Minister, Simon Coveney, says that the 'mood music' between the UK and the EU has improved but they are still 'not close to a deal'. He goes on to add that a no deal Brexit would be a 'lose-lose' situation, and would create problems 'managing civil unrest around the border'.

A leaked EU memo, circulated to ambassadors from the other 27 counties in the bloc, dismisses the UK's latest proposals to replace the backstop, saying they did not provide a 'legally operational' alternative. It says that the UK delegates 'confirmed that the proposed concepts do not amount to legally operational solutions and would have to be developed during the transition period', adding, 'the UK team further added that they would have to establish a regulatory and customs border on the island of Ireland'.

At a meeting of Labour's National Executive Committee, Momentum founder Jon Lansman proposes a motion to abolish the post of deputy leader, currently held by Tom Watson, citing the West Bromwich MP's disloyalty over Brexit.

Tom Watson tells BBC Radio 4's 'Today' programme, of the plot last night to oust him, 'these kind of things happen in Venezuela, not in UK politics'. Later in the morning, the motion to abolish the post of Deputy Leader is withdrawn after Jeremy Corbyn submits an alternative proposal which will see the post of deputy leader 'reviewed' instead. The Labour leader tells reporters, 'Tom Watson is the deputy leader of the party and I enjoy working with him', adding, 'the NEC agreed this morning that we are going to consult on the future of diversifying the deputy leadership position to reflect the diversity of our society'.

On the eve of their party conference, it is revealed that Labour's head of policy has resigned, issuing a warning that the Labour leader will not win the next General Election. Andrew Fisher, the author of the party's last manifesto, also criticises the 'blizzard of lies and excuses' from the upper echelons of the party, denouncing Mr Corbyn's team for their 'lack of professionalism, competence and human decency'.

Sunday 22nd September 2019

39 days to Brexit

As the Labour Party conference gets underway in Brighton, Jeremy Corbyn tells Andrew Marr on the BBC that he plans to go in to the next General Election promising to hold a second referendum, but refuses to say whether he would campaign for Remain or Leave. The Labour leader says, 'what we have said is that we would want to hold a consultation, a special conference of our party at the point that we have got this offer from the EU, we've got this as a remain and hopefully reform option', adding, 'I do think even those that are strongly in favour of remain would recognise the EU needs to have some reforms'. Tom Watson, Labour's deputy leader, takes a firmer stance, telling a rally, 'we are a remain party. We are a European party. We are an internationalist party. That is who we are. Not perfect, not pure. But overwhelmingly committed to Britain remaining in Europe. By backing a people's vote, by backing remain, I am sure we can deliver the Labour government the people of this country so badly need'.

In an interview broadcast on Sky News, EU President Jean-Claude Juncker insists that there would have to be border checks between Northern Ireland and the Republic. 'We have to make sure that the interests of the European Union and of the internal market will be preserved', he says, adding, 'an animal entering Northern Ireland without border control can enter without any kind of control the European Union via the southern part of the Irish island. This will not happen. We have to preserve the health and the safety of our citizens'. Mr Juncker also says that the EU 'is in no way responsible for any kind of consequences entailed by Brexit' as 'that's a British decision'.

Writing in 'The Sunday Times', Michael Gove says of the Brexit negotiations, 'if we make the wrong decisions, we will see faith in our democracy damaged. If we still find ourselves in the EU after October 31st, having accepted we can only ever leave when the EU decides and on terms it dictates, we will see support for the Conservative Party collapse'.

Ahead of the Labour Party's debate at conference tomorrow on what their Brexit policy should be, the Unite general secretary, Len McCluskey, tells Sky News, 'we must go into an election united and when we have a policy on Brexit, and Jeremy Corbyn makes it clear that that is the policy, then that is what leading members of the Shadow Cabinet should argue for. If they find that they can't argue for it because they feel strongly, well of course they have that right but they should step aside'. The Labour leader's current position, to negotiate another deal with the EU before deciding whether to back leave or remain, comes under pressure from other senior frontbenchers as well as his deputy, with shadow Foreign Secretary, Emily Thornberry, telling a fringe meeting, 'I want Jeremy to be in number 10 and my view personally is that the best chance of doing that is to speak truthfully, which is we as a party are a Remain party'. The Mayor of London, Sadiq Khan, goes further, saying in a Facebook post, 'Labour has come to a crossroads. Labour is a Remain party and we need to make this official by making it our policy to campaign to stay in the European Union under all circumstances – and to whip our MPs to back that position. It's time for Labour to commit to stopping Brexit, not only by promising to give the British public the final say, but by pledging to throw all our energy behind the campaign to stay in the European Union'.

The 'Sunday Times' reports that former porn star turned businesswoman Jennifer Arcuri was given £126,000 in public money and was treated to privileged access to three foreign trade missions led by Boris Johnson while he was Mayor of London. The allegations involve her accompanying Mr Johnson on trips to Malaysia, Singapore, New York and Tel Aviv.

Monday 23rd September 2019

38 days to Brexit

Writing in the 'Daily Mail', David Blunkett says of the current party leader, 'once again, Corbyn has let his and my party down by fomenting division and promoting extremism'. The former Labour cabinet minister goes on to add, 'no wonder long-standing members like me would wish to be anywhere other than Brighton over the next three days. If nothing changes, Labour is doomed'.

Jeremy Corbyn survives a series of votes at conference after a battle to stop members from ordering him to commit to keeping the UK in the EU. His motion was carried on a show of hands, with delegates singing 'Oh Jeremy Corbyn'. Shadow Brexit Secretary Sir Keir Starmer says, 'we had a vote. It went the way it did, obviously I am disappointed by the result', adding that it was 'obvious where the membership is on this', and that Labour would ultimately end up calling for the UK to stay in the EU. London Mayor Sadiq Khan tweets, 'I do not believe this decision reflects the views of the overwhelming majority of Labour members who desperately want to stop Brexit. Labour IS a Remain party. I will continue campaigning with @LondonLabour to give the public the final say and stop Brexit'. Jo Swinson, the Liberal Democrat leader, says, "Jeremy Corbyn has again shown a total lack of leadership on Brexit and settled on yet another fudge on the biggest issue facing our country', adding that the Labour leader 'has repeatedly had the opportunity to put the full force of the Labour Party behind a Remain position, but he has once again shown today that he is a Brexiteer at heart'.

Boris Johnson discusses Brexit with Angela Merkel, Emmanuel Macron and Donald Tusk at a series of side meetings at the UN General Assembly in New York, but reportedly makes little in the way of progress. After leaving their bilateral meeting, Mr Tusk declares that there had been 'no breakthrough' and that there is 'no time to lose' with the October 31st deadline looming.

The Supreme Court in London announces that it will deliver a verdict on the legality of the Prime Minister's prorogation of Parliament tomorrow morning at 10.30am.

Eleven Supreme Court judges unanimously find the Prime Minister's decision to prorogue Parliament unlawful. Having earlier declared the question of prorogation 'justiciable', Lady Hale, the president of the court, says, 'the decision to advise Her Majesty to prorogue Parliament was unlawful because it had the effect of frustrating or preventing the ability of Parliament to carry out its constitutional functions without reasonable justification', and was thus 'void and of no effect'. Immediately after the judgement is delivered, leaders of all of the opposition parties in Westminster call on the Prime Minister to resign. Interrupting proceedings at the Labour Party conference, Jeremy Corbyn takes to the stage to inform delegates of the Supreme Court judgement, concluding by inviting the Prime Minister to 'consider his position' and become 'the shortest-serving prime minister there has ever been'. Liberal Democrat leader Jo Swinson says Mr Johnson's actions had shown he was 'not fit to be Prime Minister' and he should resign, with Ian Blackford, leader of the SNP in Westminster, saying, 'if he doesn't go, Parliament will have to remove Boris Johnson'.

In a press conference outside the House of Commons, the Speaker, John Bercow, says, 'the citizens of the UK are entitled to expect that Parliament does discharge its core functions. I have instructed the House authorities to prepare not for the recall, prorogation was unlawful, to prepare for the resumption of the business of the house of Commons', adding that the Commons will sit again tomorrow 'and it does so at 11.30am'.

Former Prime Minister Sir John Major, who submitted written evidence in the case, responds to the judgement by saying, 'I hope this ruling from the Supreme Court will deter any future Prime Minister from attempting to shut down Parliament', adding, 'no Prime Minister must ever treat the monarch or Parliament in this way again'.

The Prime Minister, currently in New York for a meeting with President Trump, reacts to the Supreme Court ruling by telling reporters, 'we in the UK will not be deterred from delivering the will of the British people. I strongly disagree with this decision of the Supreme Court. I have the upmost respect for our judiciary but I don't think this was the right decision. I think that the prorogation has been used for centuries without this kind of challenge. Let's be in no doubt there are a lot of people who want to frustrate Brexit. There are a lot of people who want to stop this country coming out of the EU. And to be honest it is not made much easier by this kind of stuff in Parliament or in the court. But I think the most important thing is we get on and deliver Brexit on October 31st and clearly the claimants in this case are determined to frustrate that and to stop that'.

Later, the Prime Minister reaffirms his intention to leave the EU at the end of October, going on to say, 'and we will simultaneously refuse to be deterred from delivering on what I think you would all expect, an exciting, dynamic domestic agenda intended to make our country ever more attractive to live in and to invest in. So, we will be pushing on with infrastructure investment, with 20,000 police, with investing in our NHS. To do that we will need a Queen's Speech to set out what we are going to do'.

With Parliament resuming tomorrow, the Labour Party conference in Brighton is effectively cut short by one day, with Jeremy Corbyn's keynote address brought forward to this afternoon. During his speech, the Labour leader reaffirms the policy that was decided upon in the conference hall yesterday, saying, 'this crisis can only be settled with a General Election. That election needs to take place as soon as this government's threat of a disastrous no deal is taken off the table. That condition is what MPs passed into law before Boris Johnson illegally closed down Parliament. It's a protection that's clearly essential'. The Labour leader also tells the assembled delegates, 'this is an extraordinary and precarious moment in our country's history. The Prime Minister has been found to have acted illegally when he tried to shut down Parliament. The highest court in the land has found that Boris Johnson broke the law when he tried to shut down democratic accountability at a crucial moment for our public life. The Prime Minister acted illegally when he tried to shut down opposition to his reckless and disastrous plan to crash out of the European Union without a deal. But he has failed. He will never shut down our democracy or silence the voices of the people. The democracy that Boris Johnson describes as a "rigmarole" will not be stifled and the people will have their say'. Mr Corbyn goes on to repeat his message from earlier, saying, 'this unelected Prime minister should now resign'.

It is revealed that the Attorney General, Geoffrey Cox, advised the Government that their prorogation plans were 'lawful and within the constitution'. In papers previously redacted, the advice goes on to say that 'any accusations of unlawfulness were motivated by political considerations' and that the proposals were 'compatible with the provisions of the NIEF (Northern Ireland Executive Formation) Act 2019'. Sir Keir Starmer, the shadow Brexit Secretary, tells Sky News that the Attorney General 'is going to have to consider his position because he has now had a unanimous decision of the Supreme Court completely the other way'.

In reaction to the day's events, Sterling is up 0.6% against the dollar, and 0.4% up against the Euro.

Speaking to BBC Radio 4's 'Today' programme, Jeremy Corbyn denies that he is running scared of an election because of his dire popularity ratings. The Labour leader goes on to say, 'until it is very clear that the application will be made, per the legislation, to the EU to extend our membership to at least January, then we will continue pushing for that and that is our priority', adding, 'when that has been achieved we will then be ready with a motion of no confidence'.

The Liberal Democrat leader, Jo Swinson, suggests that opposition parties may seek to bring forward the date by which the Prime Minister is forced to ask the EU for an extension to Article 50. Claiming that legal efforts to compel him to act might take longer than the 12 days between the European Council summit and Brexit day on October 31st, Ms Swinson says, 'we simply cannot afford to wait until the 19th of October to see whether or not the Prime Minister will refuse to obey the law again'.

The unexpected resumption of the House of Commons begins with a statement from Geoffrey Cox, the Attorney General, on yesterday's Supreme Court ruling. Dismissing calls that he should resign, Mr Cox tells the chamber that the Supreme Court had 'made new law', something, he adds, that it was 'perfectly entitled' to do. In a sometimes heated exchange after his statement, the Attorney General mocks the opposition parties for refusing to support a General Election, saying, 'this Parliament is a dead Parliament, it has no right to sit on these green benches', before gesturing across the chamber and adding, 'this Parliament should have the courage to face the electorate. The time is coming when even these turkeys won't be able to prevent Christmas'.

Addressing the Commons after returning early from New York, Boris Johnson insists that he wants to 'honour the promise' made to voters after the referendum, and then 'move on' to 'life after Brexit'. In a noisy chamber, the Prime Minister says, 'instead of facing the voters the opposition turned tail. Instead of letting the voters decide they ran to the courts', he continues, adding that, 'this Parliament must either stand aside and let this Government get Brexit done or bring a vote of confidence and finally face the day of reckoning with the voters.' Referring to yesterday's Supreme Court ruling, the Prime Minister says, 'it's no disrespect to the judiciary to say I think the court was wrong to pronounce on what is essentially a political question at a time of great national controversy'. In response, Jeremy Corbyn dismisses his speech as '10 minutes of bluster from a dangerous Prime Minister who thinks he is above the law', going on to add that Boris Johnson is a Prime Minister who 'lacked a shred of humility' and should do the 'honourable thing' and resign.

Anger levels peak during the debate when Labour MP Paula Sheriff tells the Prime Minister that he 'should be absolutely ashamed of himself' over his Brexit rhetoric. As she speaks, she points to a commemorative shield, on the wall in the Commons chamber, to Labour MP Jo Cox who was murdered in the run up to the 2016 referendum. 'We stand here under the shield of our departed friend. Many of us in this place are subject to death threats and abuse every single day', Ms Sheriff continues, telling the Prime Minister that 'they often quote his words, Surrender Act, betrayal, traitor, and I, for one, am sick of it'. The Prime Minister responds by saying, 'I have to say that I have never heard such humbug in all my life', adding that the 'best way to honour the memory of Jo Cox, and indeed to bring this country together, would be, I think, to get Brexit done'.

Speaking to ITV later in the evening, the Prime Minister suggests that he will prorogue Parliament again in the near future. He tells Robert Peston, 'I think the public should see what we want to do and I think it's a great shame that the opposition are sort of gridlocked. They don't want either to have an election. They don't want Brexit to get done. They don't seem to want anything. So, my urging to them would be, if you seriously don't want to have an election, then let's get on with a strong domestic agenda of the kind we have'. When asked if that means he has to prorogue, the Prime Minister replies, 'we'll have to absorb the full implications of the ruling', before reaffirming, 'I would like to have a Queen's Speech'.

The Prime Minister may have earned a standing ovation from Conservative MPs in the House of Commons last night but, this morning, his words are attracting criticism. The husband of murdered MP Jo Cox tweets, 'feel a bit sick at Jo's name being used in this way', adding, 'let's all play our part in dialling it down'. Former Attorney General, Dominic Grieve, tells ITV of the reaction to the Prime Minister's performance, 'I find it terrifying actually. This is somebody who is a pathological liar, one can watch him do it in the chamber of the House of Commons', adding, 'he has no moral compass of any kind at all and it was quite deliberate, what he was saying was you do as I say and you won't be subject to death threats. That was the impact of that comment. It is total populism'. There is even thinly veiled criticism from within his own Cabinet, with Nicky Morgan, Culture Secretary, tweeting, 'I know the PM is aware of & sympathetic about the threats far too many of us have received because I shared with him recently the threats I am getting. But at a time of strong feelings we all need to remind ourselves of the effect of everything we say on those watching us.'

The Prime Minister's sister, Rachael Johnson, joins the critics, telling Sky News that her brother was 'using words like surrender, capitulation as if the people who are standing in the way of the blessed will of the people as defined by 17.4million votes in 2016 should be hung, drawn, quartered, tarred and feathered and I think that is highly reprehensible language to use'.

At a book launch in London, the Prime Minister's chief adviser, Dominic Cummings, says of Brexit, 'we are enjoying this, we are going to leave and we are going to win', adding that MPs have become 'badly disconnected' from the rest of the country. When asked about voter anger, Mr Cummings replies, 'it is not surprising some people are angry about it', adding, 'if you are a bunch of politicians and say that we swear we are going to respect the result of a democratic vote, and then after you lose you say, we don't want to respect that vote, what do you expect to happen?'

In a BBC interview, the Prime Minister defends referring to the Benn Act, which compels him to seek an extension to Article 50, as the Surrender Act. 'I do think in the House of Commons it is important I should be able to talk about the 'Surrender Bill' in the way that I did', he says, adding, 'it would take away the power of this Government and the power of this country to decide how long it would remain in the EU and give that power to the EU. That's really quite an extraordinary thing'.

Speaking at the Centre for European Reform, Sir John Major tells the audience that, 'to reinforce their electoral appeal, the Government seems intent on whipping up dissent by using highly emotional and evocative language that can only provoke fear and anger, and fuel grievances against Parliament and the law'. The former Prime Minister goes on to warn Boris Johnson that if he fails to comply fully with the Benn Act, 'it would be a piece of political chicanery that no one should ever forgive or forget'.

The Commons rejects the Government's request to suspend Parliament for three days for the Conservative Party conference, with MPs voting by 306 to 289 against a short parliamentary recess. The Government announce that the conference, which is due to start on Sunday in Manchester, will still go ahead as planned.

A joint statement from every archbishop and bishop in the Church of England condemns the language used by MPs in recent days as 'unacceptable'. 'We should speak to others with respect', the statement says, adding, 'we should not denigrate, patronise or ignore the honest views of fellow citizens but seek to respect their opinions, their participation in society, and their votes'. The Archbishop of Canterbury, Justin Welby, tells 'The Times', 'there needs to be a cooling of tempers on all sides in order to enable people to try to come to an agreement to see what solution can unite the country and do what has to be done'.

Responding to press rumours that a senior Cabinet minister has predicted civil unrest if the UK does not leave the EU on October 31st, Dominic Grieve says, 'the message coming from Downing Street is we have to leave by October 31st or there will be riots. My worry is that this is part of an orchestrated script and part of a Government policy to get around the law drafted by Labour MP Hilary Benn and approved by the Commons, with my support, designed to prevent the Prime Minister taking the UK out of the EU next month without a deal'. The former Attorney General goes on to say, 'my suspicion is that they may be planning to use the 2004 Civil Contingencies Act to suspend that law on the grounds that otherwise there will be riots before and afterwards'. His comments are described as 'shameful' by former party leader, Iain Duncan Smith, and a Downing Street spokesman dismisses the suggestion as 'utter nonsense'.

Irish deputy prime minister Simon Coveney says there are still 'significant gaps' between the EU and the UK, and that the UK has failed to put forward any 'serious' proposals. After a meeting in Brussels with Michel Barnier, Steve Barclay responds by saying, 'well, what Simon Coveney also said this week is if there's the political will, a deal can be done'. The Brexit Secretary goes on to add, 'there needs to be political will on both sides and we're now approaching the moment of truth in these negotiations.' Jean-Claude Juncker says that he and Michel Barnier are 'doing everything we can' to reach an agreement, but warns, 'if this fails in the end, the responsibility lies solely with the British side'.

The Greater London Authority's monitoring officer, who is responsible for monitoring the conduct of the London Mayor and other members of the authority, announces that he has written to the police watchdog, the Independent Office for Police Conduct, asking them to consider investigating the allegations made against Boris Johnson in last weekend's 'Sunday Times'. In a letter to the Prime Minister he says, 'the conduct matter relates to your time as Mayor of London between 2008 and 2016. During this time, it has been brought to my attention that you maintained a friendship with Ms Jennifer Arcuri and as a result of that friendship allowed Ms Arcuri to participate in trade missions and receive sponsorship monies in circumstances when she and her companies could not have expected otherwise to receive those benefits'. Responding to the referral, a Downing Street spokesman says, 'the Prime Minister, as Mayor of London, did a huge amount of work when selling our capital city around the world, beating the drum for London and the UK. Everything was done with propriety and in the normal way'. A Government spokesman describes the move, coming on the eve of the Conservative Party conference, as a 'politically motivated attack'.

In an interview published in the 'Daily Mail' today, Chancellor of the Exchequer, Sajid Javid, says of Brexit, 'we can't have this debate going on. We've had the referendum, it was the biggest democratic exercise in the history of our country. And we have to honour it'. He goes on to say, 'it's a real test of the very fabric of our democracy', adding, ''if we don't deal with this and exit on October 31st, I just fear we tear that fabric in a way that we might not be able to stitch it up again'. The Chancellor also insists that his relationship with the Prime Minister is very strong, but says of the incident which saw his aide, Sonia Khan, summarily dismissed by Dominic Cummings, 'everyone agreed that it wasn't handled well. It was agreed that there be significant changes after that. And nothing like that can ever happen again'.

SNP MP Stewart Hosie says that a move to invoke a vote of no confidence in the current Government, and then install an interim government to secure a Brexit extension, seems to be the only way to ensure that the UK did not 'crash out' of the EU on October 31st. 'We have to do that because there is now no confidence that the Prime Minister will obey the law and seek the extension that Parliament voted for only a few weeks ago', he tells the BBC Radio 4 'Today' programme. Mr Hosie goes on to say, 'if we are serious about the extension, that is the only game in town', adding that it was 'self-evidently the case' that as the leader of the second largest party Westminster, Jeremy Corbyn should have the first chance of forming an administration.

Speaking to reporters in Essex, Jeremy Corbyn says, 'our priority, all of us, is to prevent a no deal exit from the European Union'. The Labour leader goes on to say that he intends to 'make the Government carry out the EU number two act which requires them, in the event of a no deal, to apply for an extension before the 31st of October', adding, 'at that point, we're ready for an election'. Asked if he was ready to become an interim Prime Minister if necessary, Mr Corbyn replies, 'Absolutely. The normal process is that when a government collapses, the leader of the opposition is invited to form a minority government in order to carry through a specific and strictly limited process which would be to ensure no crash out and to prepare for a general election'.

The 'Sunday Times' follow up last week's story concerning Boris Johnson and American businesswoman Jennifer Arcuri with fresh allegations that the then Mayor of London was also having an affair with her. The report says that Ms Arcuri confided in university classmates and Conservative Party activists, one of whom tells the paper, 'she told me they were sleeping together'. Boris Johnson is also hit by a fresh allegation of impropriety as journalist Charlotte Edwardes accuses the Prime Minister of squeezing her thigh at a private lunch in 1999 when he was editor of the Spectator. In an article for 'Style' magazine, Ms Edwardes, who is the partner of ITV's Political Editor, Robert Peston, writes, 'under the table I feel Johnson's hand on my thigh. He gives it a squeeze. His hand is high up my leg and he has enough flesh beneath his fingers to make me sit suddenly upright'. The journalist goes on to add that after the lunch, thrown by the Spectator at their then London office, she spoke about Mr Johnson's wandering hands to another woman, who replied, 'Oh God, he did exactly the same to me'. Downing Street issues a statement saying 'this allegation is untrue', but Ms Edwardes hits back with a tweet retorting, 'If the Prime Minister doesn't recall the incident then clearly I have a better memory than he does'.

Interviewed in the 'Observer', Sir Kier Starmer addresses the suggestion that the Government could invoke the Civil Contingencies Act 2004 in a bid to avoid seeking an extension to Article 50. The shadow Brexit Secretary says, 'whipping up the idea of riots or even deaths if we do not leave the EU on 31st October is the height of irresponsibility. But it is also pretty obviously being orchestrated. If this is part of a government plan to misuse powers under emergency legislation, I can assure the PM we will defeat him in court and in Parliament'.

On the BBC, Boris Johnson dismisses the Jennifer Arcuri accusations, telling Andrew Marr that 'everything was done in accordance with the code, everything was done with full propriety'. Asked if he had declared any interest, the Prime Minister stated that 'there was no interest to declare', adding that the current Mayor, Sadiq Khan, 'could possibly spend more time investing in police officers than he is investing in press officers and peddling this kind of stuff'.

The Conservative Party conference gets underway in Manchester with Jacob Rees-Mogg saying of the Brexit process, 'like Gulliver tied down at Lilliput, we are tied down by a ragtag, motley collection of feeble, fickle, footling politicians. All in desperate pursuit of a single ignoble aim, to renege on the solemn promise they made to the British people and try to cancel the largest single democratic mandate in our history'. The Leader of the House of Commons also criticises John Bercow saying that, although he has great respect for the Speaker, his 'recent mistakes' have 'damaged the standing of the House in the eyes of the British public to the lowest point in modern history'. Later, Dominic Raab warns delegates not to put Jeremy Corbyn in to Downing Street. 'I say this as a passionate Brexiteer, there are some things even bigger than Brexit', the Foreign Secretary says, adding, 'so, to any of our colleagues, or former colleagues, tempted to put Jeremy Corbyn and his momentum mob into No 10, as part of some temporary anti-Brexit coalition, I just say this: history would never forgive you'.

The SNP's Westminster leader, Ian Blackford, calls for opposition parties to unite and bring down the Government this week to install a caretaker Prime Minister who would delay Brexit, saying that it was not enough to 'sit back and hope Boris Johnson doesn't allow us to crash out without a deal', adding, 'we do not believe Johnson is going to extend Article 50, and we won't risk time running out'.

Mary Wakefield, a journalist at the Spectator magazine and an employee of Boris Johnson's during his time as editor, issues a statement regarding Charlotte Edwardes accusations yesterday. Ms Wakefield, who is married to the Prime Minister's senior advisor, Dominic Cummings, says, 'Boris was a good boss and nothing like this ever happened to me. Nor has Charlotte, who I like and admire, ever discussed the incident with me'. Chancellor, Sajid Javid, says that he 'totally trusts' the Prime Minister over the allegations, but Health Secretary, Matt Hancock, says of Ms Edwardes, 'I know her and I know her to be trustworthy'. Former Work and Pensions Secretary Amber Rudd, who quit the Tories and now sits as an independent MP, says in a tweet, 'I agree with Matt Hancock'.

Opposition parties meet in London, but the talks break up with no sign of agreement on their next move. The SNP's Westminster leader Ian Blackford insists the group are 'united' against no deal, but admits there was no prospect of an imminent confidence vote despite he himself urging one over the weekend. Jo Swinson says of Jeremy Corbyn becoming caretaker Prime Minister, 'he simply does not have the numbers.' Caroline Lucas, the leader of the Green Party says, 'I don't think anyone is expecting a vote of no confidence this week'.

At the Conservative Party conference in Manchester, Sajid Javid says of the October 31st Brexit deadline, 'we are leaving the European Union. It's not a matter of if, it's a matter of days, 31 days, deal or no deal', adding, 'we're ready to draw on the full armoury of economic policy if needed'.

Tuesday 1st October 2019

30 days to Brexit

At the Conservative Party conference, Home Secretary, Priti Patel, promises to 'end the free movement of people once and for all' after Brexit, adding, 'instead we will introduce an Australian style points-based immigration system. One that works in the best interests of Britain'.

Asked directly, during an interview with Beth Rigby on Sky News, whether he had an affair with American businesswoman Jennifer Arcuri, Boris Johnson replies, 'I've said what I have to say about that matter'. Pressing him further, Ms Rigby says, 'the reason I ask...I don't want to talk about your private life. It's about whether you misused public money, that's why I'm asking if you were having a sexual relationship?' The Prime Minister answers, 'I can certainly say there was absolutely no question of that at all'. When asked about Ms Arcuri on the BBC, the Prime Minister replies, 'quite a few people don't want Brexit to be done and I think rightly or wrongly they conceive of me as the person who is helping to deliver Brexit and it is inevitable that I am going to come under a certain amount of shot and shell. I don't mind that in the least'.

The EU's incoming trade commissioner, Phil Hogan, says that EU leaders believe another extension beyond October 31st is now more likely than striking a deal. He says, 'there's been a lot of activity on Brexit in the last three years and they're wondering when the next extension's coming because inevitably that's the way things are developing'. Mr Hogan goes on to suggest that time is running short for any new agreement, saying, 'we're talking about ten days to do a deal and it doesn't always happen that quickly around here', adding, 'the kamikaze way this is now being dealt with by the UK Government is not something we've chosen'.

Government sources confirm that Boris Johnson will reveal his plan for a Brexit deal with the EU tomorrow.

In his keynote speech to the Conservative Party conference, the Prime Minister describes Parliament as a 'pebble in the shoe' of the nation, saying, 'if it was a school it would have been shut down by Ofsted'. On Brexit, he says, 'we will under no circumstances have checks at or near the border in Northern Ireland', adding, 'we will respect the peace process and the Good Friday agreement. And by a process of renewable democratic consent by the executive and assembly of Northern Ireland we will go further and protect the existing regulatory arrangements for farmers and other businesses on both sides of the border'. Boris Johnson goes on to tell delegates, 'at the same time we will allow the UK, whole and entire, to withdraw from the EU, with control of our own trade policy from the start, and to protect the union', declaring his plan a 'compromise by the UK' and adding, 'I hope very much that our friends understand that and compromise in their turn'.

Boris Johnson reveals the Government's proposal to replace the backstop in a letter to EU President Jean-Claude Juncker, challenging him to accept a 'reasonable compromise' and warning that the only alternative is no deal. The five-point plan consists of:

1. Northern Ireland leaving the Customs' Union with the rest of the UK but staying in the single market. This would constitute an 'all island regulatory zone' that covers trade of all goods. It would mean no checks between the two nations, because Northern Ireland would still have to follow EU rules. Goods from Britain to Northern Ireland would effectively be managed by a border in the Irish Sea, with checks only in that direction, not the reverse.

2. A Stormont Lock. The 'all island regulatory zone' will have to be approved by the people of Northern Ireland. This means the Northern Ireland Assembly has the right to veto the zone and could hold a referendum on the matter.

3. Customs checks would have to be put in place on trade between Northern and the Republic of Ireland. Most checks would be made using technology, but some would still have to be physical.

4. A promise of a 'new deal for Northern Ireland' meaning ministers putting money aside for Belfast and Dublin to aide economic development and ensure that the new measures work.

5. Keeping to the Good Friday agreement by allowing freedom of movement between the two countries to continue.

Mr Juncker responds quickly, acknowledging some 'positive advances' in the proposal, but warning that there were still some 'problematic points', whilst Irish Prime Minister, Leo Varadkar, declares that it does 'not fully meet the agreed objectives' and did not look like the 'basis for an agreement'. Guy Verhofstadt, head of the European Parliament's Brexit Steering Group, suggests the UK offer was not a serious attempt at reaching a deal but an effort to shift blame for failure to Brussels, adding, 'the first assessment of nearly every member in the BSG was not positive at all'. Michel Barnier, the EU's chief negotiator, is reported as saying of the plan, 'the EU would then be trapped with no backstop to preserve the single market after Brexit'.

Response at home is more positive, with DUP leader Arlene Foster immediately hailing the five point blueprint as 'a serious and sensible' way forward which 'allows the people of Northern Ireland a role which they didn't have'. The chairman of the European Research Group, Steve Baker, describes the plan as 'fair and reasonable', while veteran Eurosceptic Tory John Redwood says he was 'very pleased' with Mr Johnson's decision to abandon Mrs May's plan to keep the UK closely aligned with the EU. Labour MP Stephen Kinnock suggests that up to 30 of his colleagues could be persuaded to back the plans if Mr Johnson can strike a deal with Brussels, saying, 'if Dublin and Brussels are happy, then we're happy'. Responding to the initial reactions, Michael Gove tells ITV's Robert Peston, 'that seems to me to be a pretty solid majority'. Jeremy Corbyn, however, is more reticent, telling Sky News, 'I think the very least he could do is come to the House of Commons tomorrow to explain what his proposals are and to answer questions on them. We will be able to tell him quite clearly that we believe this deal is not acceptable. We do believe that a much better deal can be reached with the European Union'.

A new opinion poll, conducted by YouGov, puts the Liberal Democrats in second place on 23 percent, with Labour in third, two points behind the Lib Dems. The Conservative Party remain unchanged on 34 percent. The poll puts the Brexit Party on 12 percent, one point better than it recorded on September 3rd, with the Green Party in fifth place on 5 percent.

The Government announce that Parliament is to be prorogued again from next week, with a Downing Street statement saying, 'the Prime Minister has been consistently clear that he wants to set out a fresh legislative programme in a Queen's Speech. He therefore intends to request that the current session of Parliament be prorogued from the evening of Tuesday October 8th, with a Queen's Speech on Monday October 14th'.

Boris Johnson presents his Brexit plans to the House of Commons saying, 'they do not deliver everything we would have wished. They do represent a compromise. But to remain a prisoner of existing positions is to become a cause of deadlock rather than breakthrough and so we have made a genuine attempt to bridge the chasm, to reconcile the apparently irreconcilable and to go the extra mile as time runs short'. The Prime Minister reinforces that the 'government's objective has always been to leave with a deal', but warns 'if our European neighbours choose not to show a corresponding willingness to reach a deal than we shall have to leave on October the 31st without an agreement, and we are ready to do so'. In response, Jeremy Corbyn says, 'no Labour MP could support such a reckless deal that will be used as a springboard to attack rights and standards in this country', adding that the Government want 'a Trump-deal Brexit that would crash our economy and rip away the standards that put a floor under people's rights at work, that protect our environment and protect our consumers'.

The Prime Minister's proposal is met with praise from a number of Eurosceptic Conservative MPs, with Bill Cash 'welcoming indications of progress in these negotiations' and Sir Graham Brady saying that he believed the plan fulfilled the terms of his amendment from earlier in the year, still the only Brexit framework that has been passed by the Commons. The plan is not greeted so warmly in Ireland, however, with Deputy Prime Minister, Simon Coveney, saying, 'if that is the final proposal, there will be no deal', and Leo Varadkar reaffirming that the proposal did not form the 'basis for an agreement'. Asked about the possibility of the UK staying in the EU, the Irish Prime Minister replies, 'all the polls since Prime Minister Johnson became Prime Minister suggest that's what the British people actually want, but their political system isn't able to give them that choice'. The Taoiseach goes on to say, 'our objective is very clear, we don't want to see any customs posts between north and south nor do we want to see any tariffs or restrictions on trade between north and south. They were all abolished in the 1990s and we don't want to go back to that. The majority of the people in the north don't and the majority of the people in the Republic of Ireland don't'.

The Irish Prime Minister's remarks cause anger in London, with Conservative MP Peter Bone saying that the comments from Mr Varadkar were 'extraordinary' and 'meddling'. Fellow Tory MP Nigel Evans says, 'the British people voted to leave the EU. We are democrats in the UK and we have never ignored a result of a referendum unlike other EU countries including Ireland'. DUP deputy leader Nigel Dodds accuses Mr Varadkar of 'a clear ramping up of rhetoric designed to derail any realistic prospect of a deal', going on to say, 'the flippant Dublin reaction to the Prime Minister's proposals has also exposed the reality that the Irish government would never have consented to the United Kingdom leaving the backstop if it had been implemented'.

A statement from the EU Brexit Steering Group says, 'safeguarding peace and stability on the island of Ireland, protection of citizens and the EU's legal order has to be the main focus of any deal. The UK proposals do not match even remotely what was agreed as a sufficient compromise in the backstop'. The group's head, Guy Verhofstadt, says it would be 'nearly impossible' to get approval from MEPs

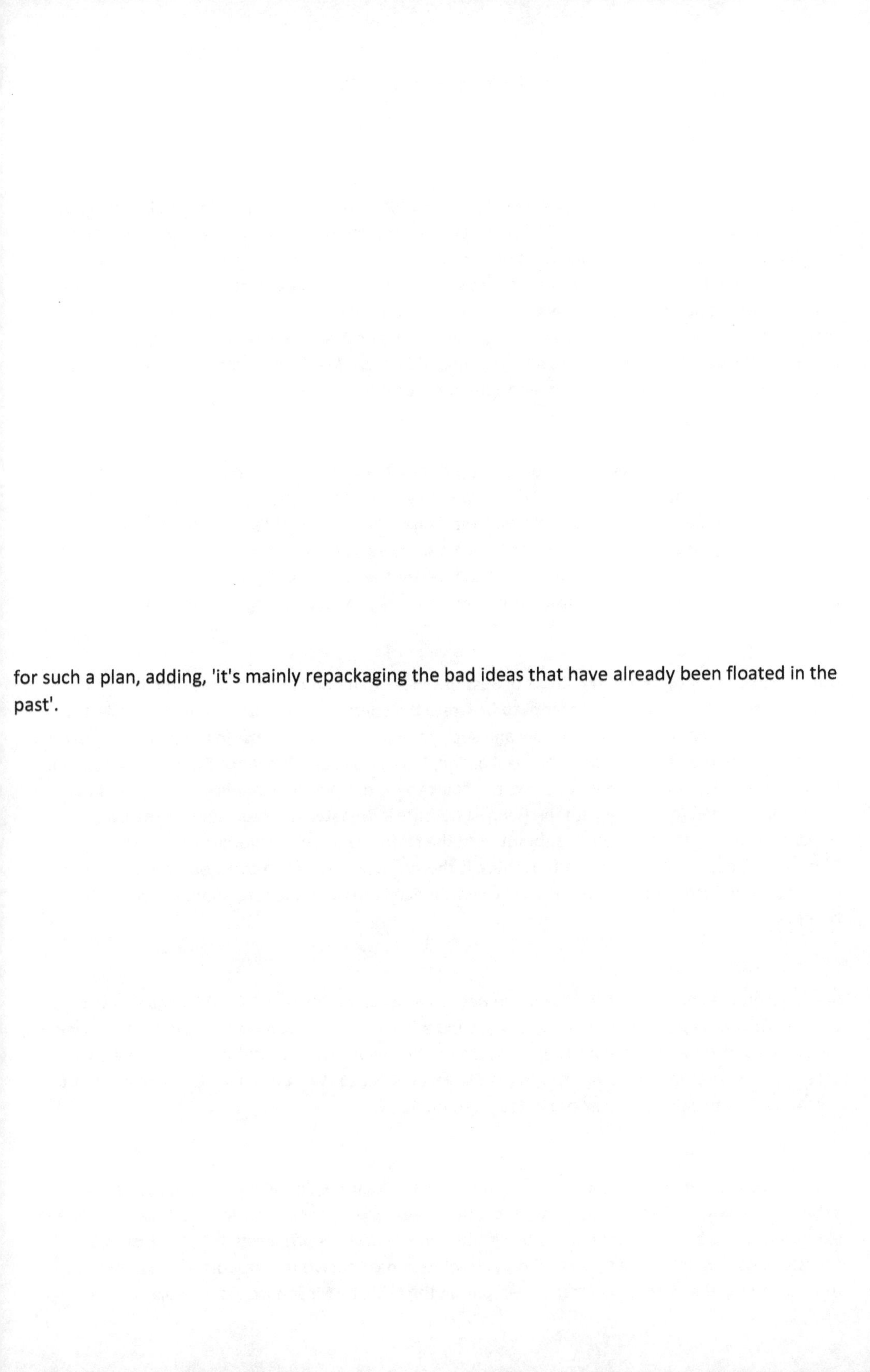

for such a plan, adding, 'it's mainly repackaging the bad ideas that have already been floated in the past'.

In an article for 'The Sun' newspaper, Conservative MEP Daniel Hannan says that he is 'not optimistic' that the EU will accept the Prime Minister's alternative to the backstop. Mr Hannan writes, 'my hunch is that Brussels will still say no. Why? Because, for the EU, the aim was never to avoid a hard border in Ireland — something these proposals plainly achieve. The aim, rather, was to keep Britain in a subordinate position, still subject to EU law and trade policy'. He supports his assertion by referencing a fly-on-the-wall documentary screened earlier this year in which a member of Guy Verhofstadt's negotiating team was filmed saying of Theresa May's acceptance of the backstop, 'it took us two years, but we finally turned them into a colony'.

The Prime Minister's chief Brexit negotiator, David Frost, and his team of Downing Street officials fail to win their EU counterparts approval during meetings over the proposed alternative to the backstop. A European commission spokeswoman says, 'we have completed discussions with the UK for today. We gave our initial reaction to the UK's proposals and asked many questions on the legal text. We will meet again on Monday to give the UK another opportunity to present its proposals in detail'. She adds that the proposals do not 'provide a basis for concluding an agreement'.

Documents are submitted to the Court of Sessions in Scotland on behalf of the Prime Minister making it clear that he will not attempt to frustrate the so-called Benn Act. The papers state that the Prime Minister will comply with the law and seek an extension if he is unable to strike an agreement with the EU before 19th October. The legal action, led by businessman Vince Dale, SNP MP Joanna Cherry QC and Jolyon Maugham QC, asks the court to lay out potential punishments should the Prime Minister fail to comply with the Benn Act. Andrew Webster QC, representing the UK Government, says the documents submitted to the court are a 'clear statement' as to what the Prime Minister will do, going on to argue that there is therefore no need for a court order because the court has it on record that the letter will be sent. Judge Lord Pentland is to announce his decision on Monday.

Steve Baker, the chairman of the European Research Group of Conservative MPs, appears to suggest that the Government could still find a way around a delay as he responds to the court case, tweeting, 'A source confirms all this means is that government will obey the law. It does not mean we will extend. It does not mean we will stay in the EU beyond Oct 31. We will leave.' Boris Johnson also take to twitter to say, 'New deal or no deal - but no delay.'

Leo Varadkar, the Irish Taoiseach, says during a visit to Denmark, 'if the UK were to request an extension, we would consider it, most EU countries would only consider it for good reason, but an extension would be better than no deal'. Of the Prime Minister's proposed deal, the Irish Prime Minister says, 'I'm interested in solutions, any solution has to have the support of the people of Ireland and Northern Ireland. What's been put on the table by Mr Johnson is not supported by business or civil society in Northern Ireland, it's only supported by one political party, so there's a long way to go'.

Rory Stewart, a contender for the Conservative Party leadership in July but now one of the 21 Tory rebels who have had the whip removed, announces that he will be standing down at the next election and has resigned from the party. In a tweet, the former International Development Secretary thanks his Penrith constituents before announcing that he intends to run as an independent candidate in the 2020 London Mayoral Elections.

Dutch Prime Minister Mark Rutte adds his voice to those expressing scepticism at Boris Johnson's plans for a deal with the EU, saying 'important questions remain' about the Prime Minister's proposals. Speaking after a phone call with Mr Johnson, he says, 'there is a lot of work to be done ahead of October 17/18'.

A source close to Guy Verhofstadt, the head of the EU's Brexit Steering Group, says, 'Boris Johnson's proposal does not have a chance. He seems to be gunning for no deal. Nothing is moving at all this weekend'.

Margot James, one of the 21 Tory rebels expelled from the party last month, tells BBC Radio 4's 'The Week in Westminster' that she thought she and the other sacked rebels would be able to support the proposals. 'If the Prime Minister can get EU and Irish agreement then I think that we would, we've all got reservations, but we would be prepared to compromise and vote for the deal', the former Digital Minister says, adding, 'our prime concern really is to avoid Britain leaving without a deal'. Labour MP Lisa Nandy, whose Wigan constituency voted comprehensively to leave, tells the same programme, 'the truth is we're further away from a deal than we were two months ago and I can't see this getting anywhere'.

Writing in 'The Sun' newspaper, the Prime Minister says, 'we will be packing our bags and walking out on October 31st', adding, 'the only question is whether Brussels cheerily waves us off with a mutually agreeable deal, or whether we will be forced to head off on our own'. Boris Johnson goes on to say, 'regrettably, there are some MPs — led, unsurprisingly, by that serial wannabe Brexit-wrecker Jeremy Corbyn — who have said they will oppose this deal in any circumstances', but goes on to praise the 'spirit of compromise from MPs on all sides who have looked at what's on the table, reflected on what's best for their constituents, and decided they are willing to put aside their personal beliefs and back the deal that they know will get Brexit done'.

Speaking at an event organised by 'Le Monde' newspaper, Michel Barnier, says of Boris Johnson's proposal, 'if they do not change, I do not believe, on the basis of the mandate I have been given by the EU27, that we can advance'. The EU's chief negotiator also says, 'we are ready for no deal, even if we don't desire it. No deal will never be the choice of the EU. If it happens, it would be Britain's choice'.

Sunday 6th October 2019

25 days to Brexit

In a telephone call with President Macron, Boris Johnson tells the French leader that the EU should not be lured into the mistaken belief that the UK will stay in the EU after October 31st, and urges the EU to 'match the compromises' the UK has made. A senior No 10 source adds, 'the Surrender Act and its authors are undermining negotiations, but if EU leaders are betting that it will prevent no deal, that would be an historic misunderstanding'. In turn, an official at the Élysée Palace says of the conversation, 'the President told him that the negotiations should continue swiftly with Michel Barnier's team in coming days, in order to evaluate at the end of the week whether a deal is possible that respects European Union principles'.

It is announced that ex-Tory Dominic Grieve will be given a free run by the Lib Dems at the next General Election, paving the way for him to stand as a Remain Alliance candidate. The former Attorney General, now an independent, says, 'it's up to other political parties to decide whether they wish to put up a candidate. My understanding is that the Liberal Democrats will decide not to do so, for which I am grateful. I believe that will be helpful'.

Baroness Chakrabarti, the shadow Attorney General, tells Andrew Marr on the BBC that the so called Benn Act 'was drafted with great care after a great deal of co-operation across the House of Commons and it is very, very specific and explicit about the personal duty on the Prime Minister to either get a deal through the House of Commons or persuade the House of Commons that no deal is plausible, or he has to write a letter. The letter has been drafted and attached to the Act to the European Union asking for more time'. She says of Boris Johnson, 'he seems to have a very casual relationship with the law. He seems to think he is above the law. As the Supreme Court showed us a few weeks ago, he is not. No one is above the law, even a British Prime Minister'.

Speaking to Sky New's Sophie Ridge, Housing Secretary Robert Jenrick says that the UK would be leaving the EU on October 31st and 'we've said that, as any Government would do, we will comply with the law'. When pressed on the issue of the requirements of the Benn Act, Mr Jenrick replies, 'the Prime Minister has been very clear that he is not going to extend Article 50, I don't think he personally could have been any clearer'.

A poll by Opinium for the 'Observer' newspaper puts the Conservatives on 38 percent with Labour on 23 and the Lib Dems dropping to 15 percent. The Brexit Party holds steady on 12 percent.

Jennifer Arcuri gives an exclusive interview to 'Good Morning Britain' but refuses to answer host Piers Morgan's questions about whether she had an affair with Boris Johnson, despite being asked six times. Ms Arcuri admits he came to her flat 'around five times' but insists, 'I am not going to be putting myself in a position for you to weaponise my answer. Boris had nothing to do with my other achievements'. Later in the day, the Prime Minister refuses to answer questions about Ms Arcuri's interview, telling Sky News, during a visit to Watford General Hospital, 'I've said all I am going to say about that'.

The legal action in the Scottish Court of Session, requesting that the court lay out potential punishments should the Prime Minister not comply with the Benn Act, fails. Judge Lord Pentland says in his judgement it was neither necessary nor appropriate 'to make the order because representatives of the government had already accepted it would abide by the law'. However, the court delivered a warning to the Prime Minister, saying it would be 'destructive to the core principles of the constitution' if he reneges on his commitments.

Businesses could be hit with an annual £15bn bill for filling in customs forms for trade between the UK and the EU in the event of a no deal Brexit, according to a British government paper published today. Companies in the UK and EU would face 'a significant new and ongoing administrative burden' if Britain were to crash out of the bloc, the assessment by HM Revenue & Customs warns.

The leaders of the opposition parties in Westminster meet again but fail to agree on a cohesive way forward, with Jeremy Corbyn still insisting that he should be caretaker Prime Minister should the Government be defeated in a vote of no confidence. After the meeting, Liberal Democrat leader Jo Swinson says, 'Liberal Democrats are absolutely prepared to go forward with a government of national unity,' but warns that, 'Jeremy Corbyn doesn't have the numbers to command a majority and until he accepts that fact he could end up being the biggest block to stopping a no deal Brexit'. SNP leader Nicola Sturgeon tweets, 'Both Labour and the Lib Dems need to grow up. Who leads a temporary govt that will be in office for just a matter of days is not the key issue. What matters is getting this Tory government out, securing an extension and then having a General Election ASAP.'

Heidi Allen joins the Liberal Democrats, claiming that at least 20 'one-nation Tories' are ready to follow suit. The former Conservative MP, who quit the party early this year to form the Independent Group, which later renamed to Change UK, before sitting as an independent, says, 'the party I joined doesn't exist anymore' and has turned in to 'Ukip or Brexit Party Mark 2'. She goes on to add that by, 'shifting to the extremes, the Conservatives and Labour have turned their backs on the liberal, progressive centre ground our country is crying out for'.

A series of No. 10 briefings claim that the German Chancellor, Angela Merkel, has made it clear that a Brexit deal is now 'overwhelmingly unlikely'. Number 10 sources say that Mrs Merkel told the Prime Minister, during a 30-minute telephone call, that Northern Ireland must remain within the EU's customs union indefinitely. It is reported that Boris Johnson replied that her position meant a deal was 'essentially impossible, not just now but ever'. The Downing Street source went on to declare that the call between the two leaders was a 'clarifying moment'.

The comments from Downing Street are met with a quick response from the EU, with Council President, Donald Tusk, tweeting the Prime Minister directly to say, 'What's at stake is not winning some stupid blame game. At stake is the future of Europe and the UK as well as the security and interests of our people. You don't want a deal, you don't want an extension, you don't want to revoke, quo vadis?'. Jean-Claude Juncker says that if negotiations fail, 'the explanation will be found in the British camp', adding, 'the original sin is found on the islands and not on the continent'.

Arlene Foster also reacts angrily to the reports, saying, 'the comments from the German Chancellor to the Prime Minister that Northern Ireland must remain in the EU Customs Union forever now reveal the real objective of Dublin and the European Union. For the United Kingdom to be asked to leave a part of its sovereign territory in a foreign organisation of which the UK would no longer be a part and over which we would have no say whatsoever is beyond crazy. No UK Government could ever concede such a surrender'. The leader of the DUP goes on to say, 'the true purpose of the backstop is now in the open for all to see', adding, 'it was neither temporary nor an insurance policy'.

Shadow Brexit Secretary, Sir Keir Starmer, takes a different view, saying, 'this is yet another cynical attempt by No 10 to sabotage the negotiations'. He goes on to add, 'Boris Johnson will never take responsibility for his own failure to put forward a credible deal. His strategy from day one has been for a no deal Brexit. It is now more important than ever that Parliament unites to prevent this reckless government crashing us out of the EU at the end of the month'.

Leo Varadkar tells RTE news, 'there are some fundamental objectives that haven't changed for the past three years and we need them guaranteed'. The Irish Prime Minister goes on to add, 'I think it is going to be very difficult to secure an agreement by next week, quite frankly. Essentially what the United Kingdom has done is repudiate the deal that we negotiated in good faith with Prime Minister May's government over two years and sort of put half of that now back on the table saying, 'That's a concession'. And, of course, it isn't really'.

Parliament is prorogued this evening, bringing to an end the longest Parliamentary session in UK history. The Houses will reconvene on Monday for the Queen's Speech.

Guy Verhofstadt launches a blistering attack on Boris Johnson in the European Parliament, with the EU's Brexit co-ordinator telling MEPs, 'all those who are not playing his game are traitors, or collaborators, or surrenderers. Well, in my opinion, dear colleagues, the real traitor is he or she who would risk bringing disaster upon his country, its economy, its citizens by pushing Britain out of the European Union. That is, in my opinion, a traitor'. Jean-Claude Juncker tells MEPs, 'personally, I don't exclude a deal. Michel and myself are working on a deal', whilst Michel Barnier says, 'we will be available 24/7 in the upcoming days to try and reach an agreement. I think if there is goodwill on all sides, an agreement is still possible'.

Ahead of proposed talks with the Prime Minister later in the week, Leo Varadkar says, 'I think that the proposal that Boris Johnson exactly one week ago has put forward was not serious at all. Not serious at all because it was in fact, I call it a virtual proposal, it was not a real proposal. It gives, in fact, a veto to the DUP in a number of issues.' The Irish Prime Minister goes on to say, 'the real reason why this is all happening is very simple. It's a blame game. A blame game against everybody. A blame game against the union, against Ireland, against Mrs Merkel, against the British judiciary system, against Labour, against the Lib Dems, even against Mrs May. The only one who is not being blamed is Mr Johnson himself apparently, but all the rest are the source of our problems'.

Former Foreign Secretary, Jeremy Hunt, writes to all EU foreign ministers to warn them they are on the brink of a 'catastrophic miscalculation' in their handling of Brexit. Mr Hunt says that the EU made two mistakes when it failed to offer more generous terms during negotiations with David Cameron and Theresa May, adding, 'now it appears that the EU is about to make a third'. Speaking to the 'Daily Mail', Mr Hunt goes further, saying, 'a no deal could easily sour relations between the UK and the EU for a generation, and I think that would be a tragedy on both sides. I think it's a profound historic mistake to allow this to happen when it clearly doesn't need to'.

Boris Johnson and Leo Varadkar hold three hours of talks at Thornton Manor on the Wirral, a meeting which the Irish Prime Minister describes afterwards as 'very positive'. 'I think it is possible for us to come to an agreement, to have a treaty agreed, to allow the UK to leave the EU in an orderly fashion and to have that done by the end of October', the Taoiseach says, adding, 'in terms of concessions, I don't think this should be seen in the context of who's making concessions or who the winners or losers are'.

News emerges that Remainer MPs are planning to force a second referendum bill through Parliament before a General Election. Labour MP Hilary Benn tells BBC 'Newsnight', 'we have shown our capacity to take control of the order paper, so we won't be waiting just to see what the Prime Minister has in store for us. This is a big opportunity for Parliament to say we can find a way forward and a confirmatory referendum is the way to do it'. Margot James, a former Tory MP who was expelled for opposing no deal, indicates she would also back a second vote. 'It is vital that this time we actually do something concrete', she says, adding, 'I could support the Theresa May deal with a confirmatory referendum'. Speaking in Northampton, Jeremy Corbyn says he still wants an election, followed by a referendum if Labour wins. He adds that avoiding no deal was the 'absolute priority' but confirms that, 'after an election a Labour government would introduce legislation to ensure a referendum'. His position is contradicted by shadow Foreign Secretary Emily Thornberry, who says, 'my concern about a General Election is it would be a kind of quasi-referendum, that it would be all about in or out, what kind of deal, and so to a certain extent I can see the sense in trying to have a referendum first'.

Friday 11th October 2019

20 days to Brexit

Following the optimistic tones of yesterday's meeting between Leo Varadkar and Boris Johnson, the European Union give the go ahead for a weekend of intense negotiations aimed at hammering out a Brexit agreement ahead of the EU summit next Thursday. The Prime Minister welcomes the announcement, but warns that 'there's a way to go' and that it is not yet a 'done deal', adding, 'it's important now that our negotiators on both sides get into proper talks about how to sort this thing out'. Although details of the new blueprint discussed by the two leaders have not been published, EU sources suggest that the breakthrough has been secured by the Prime Minister agreeing to a customs border in the Irish Sea. Speaking on a visit to a school, the Prime Minister would only say that the new proposal means the 'whole of the UK takes full advantage of Brexit'. When pressed on the question of whether Northern Ireland will definitely leave the EU's customs union, Boris Johnson replies that people should simply 'look at what I have said before and draw their own conclusions'.

Responding to the Prime Minister's words, DUP leader Arlene Foster insists that her party could not support anything that 'traps Northern Ireland in the European Union, whether single market or customs union, as the rest of the UK leaves', but adds that she was willing to be 'flexible' and indicated she could support proposals that see Northern Ireland treated differently to the rest of the UK as long as they have the backing of people in the province.

On a visit to Cyprus Donald Tusk says, 'a week ago I told PM Johnson that if there was no such proposal by today, I would announce publicly that there are no more chances – because of objective reasons - for a deal during the incoming European Council'. The EU Council President goes on to say, 'however, yesterday, when the Irish Taoiseach and the UK Prime Minister met, they both saw - for the first time - a pathway to a deal'.

Dominic Grieve insists that the Prime Minister will have to accept a delay to Brexit even if his deal is passed by Parliament. The former Attorney General says, 'he's going to have to extend. I cannot see how he would be justified in trying to force through a major piece of constitutional legislation, the Withdrawal Agreement Act, in seven days. It's improper.' His comments are supported by former Cabinet Office Minister Sir David Lidington who says, 'I've always felt there would at least need to be a time where technical legal details had to be hammered out and that was going to take us beyond the end of October'.

The Mayor of London, Sadiq Khan, again calls for Jeremy Corbyn to back a second referendum before a General Election. Mr Khan tells the 'Guardian', 'I am not sure, bearing in mind how big Brexit is, that we can have a General Election and argue on NHS, policing, schools, the environment with Brexit not being resolved and our position being so unclear; it's bad politics and the wrong place for us to be'.

Sir Kier Starmer warns of legal action against the Prime Minister should he attempt to push a no deal Brexit through Parliament. Speaking to the 'Sun' newspaper, the shadow Brexit Secretary says, 'if he can't – or I should say won't – get a deal we will take whatever steps are necessary to prevent our country crashing out of the EU without a deal. If no deal is secured by this time next week, Boris Johnson must seek and accept an extension. That's the law. No ifs, no buts. And if he doesn't, we'll enforce the law – in the courts and in Parliament. Whatever it takes, we will prevent a no deal Brexit'.

Sunday 13th October 2019

18 days to Brexit

Writing in the 'Sunday Telegraph', Jacob Rees-Mogg says, 'in the final stages of the Brexit negotiation, compromise will inevitably be needed, something even the staunchest leavers recognise albeit unwillingly - but as a leaver, Boris can be trusted'. The Leader of the Commons goes on to say, 'he wants to take back control and has dedicated his political career to this noble cause. If he thinks the ship of state is worth an extra ha'porth of tar he deserves support'.

During a cabinet conference call, the Prime Minister tells his colleagues that if MPs who are against no deal now oppose his new deal they will be 'exposing their true aim of wanting to stop Brexit altogether'.

Rebecca Long-Bailey, who has up until now been a strong opponent of a second referendum, says she would now back a public vote on a deal. The shadow Business Secretary tells the BBC's 'Andrew Marr Show', 'I think the only option we've got now is to let the people decide. I know many colleagues are of a similar opinion to me'. Her leader, however, in an interview with Sky News's Sophie Ridge, appears to disagree. When asked whether any deal secured by the Prime Minister should be put to a referendum, Jeremy Corbyn replies, 'I think many in Parliament, not necessarily Labour MPs but others, might be inclined to support it, because they don't really agree with the deal – but I would caution them on this'. Scottish First Minister Nicola Sturgeon says she doubts whether any caretaker government could be sustained long enough to push through the legislation required for a referendum, adding, 'I question whether it will be possible for the opposition parties to come together'. Her point is reinforced when Jo Swinson is asked if there were any circumstances in which should could support Jeremy Corbyn as a caretaker Prime Minister, the Liberal Democrat leader replying emphatically, 'No. Jeremy Corbyn is not fit to be PM'.

In a briefing to EU diplomats, Michel Barnier says that there has not been 'as much progress' as hoped in the intense discussions that have taken place this weekend, and warns that it will be 'very difficult' to reach a new Brexit deal by the October 31st deadline.

A new parliamentary session begins with a Queen's Speech containing 26 Bills, seven of which relate to crime and justice issues, but commentators point out that none of the Bills being put forward are likely to become law, given the Government is around 40 votes short of a majority and an election is potentially looming. In a statement accompanying the speech, the Prime Minister says that 'people are tired of stasis, gridlock and waiting for change', adding, 'and they don't want to wait any longer to get Brexit done and to answer that clarion call of 17.4 million people in the greatest exercise of democracy in our national history'.

Speaking in the Commons after the State Opening of Parliament, Jeremy Corbyn says, 'there has never been such a farce as a Government with a majority of minus 45 and a 100 per cent record of defeat in the House of Commons setting out a legislative agenda they know cannot be delivered in this Parliament'. Responding to cries that he should allow an election, the Labour leader says, 'I said to the PM last month, get the extension, take us away from the dangers of no deal and then we are in a position to do that', adding, 'we may be just weeks away from the first Queen's Speech of a Labour Government'.

Simon Coveney, the Irish Deputy Prime Minister, tells reporters that he believes 'a deal is possible' and that an accord 'may even be possible this week'. However, he also warns that 'we're not there yet' and that time is running out ahead of a meeting of European leaders in Brussels at the end of the week. Finnish Prime Minister Antti Rinne, whose country holds the EU's rolling presidency, says, 'I think there is no time in a practical or legal way to find an agreement before the EU council meeting. We need more time'.

Talks continue between the Government and the EU, but even if a deal is reached it is not certain to get through Parliament. Former Home Secretary Amber Rudd tells the 'Independent', 'my concern with the proposal, let's not call it a deal yet, the proposal that we have at the moment, is that there is no sign of a level playing field, of regulatory alignment for rest of the country outside of Northern Ireland. That will hit manufacturing, so I'm concerned about that element of it'. Ms Rudd says she would wait to see the details of the political declaration adding, 'I'm not giving unconditional support'. Former Northern Ireland Secretary, Owen Paterson, tells the 'Sun', 'concerns remain that the EU will seek to trap Northern Ireland permanently in the EU Customs Union by trying to reheat the failed ideas of customs partnerships or single customs territories that proved so disastrous for Theresa May. We await the full details of the new deal to see exactly how they address the objections to the dead Theresa May deal, but dual-tariff systems like this would be, as Priti Patel has said, unacceptable'.

Commenting on the ongoing negotiations, Donald Tusk says, 'it is still undergoing changes and the basic foundations of this agreement are ready and theoretically we could accept a deal tomorrow. Yesterday evening I was ready to bet on it, today again certain doubts have appeared from the British side. Everything is going in the right direction, but you will have noticed yourselves that with Brexit and above all with our British partners anything is possible'.

Speaking in Ireland this morning, Leo Varadkar suggests the chances of an agreement are improving. 'There is a pathway to a possible deal but there are many issues that still need to be fully resolved, particularly around the consent mechanism and also some issues around customs and VAT', he says, adding, 'I spoke to the Prime Minister by phone this morning and I have also been in contact with the European Commission and I do think we are making progress but there are issues yet to be resolved and hopefully that can be done today. But if it's not, there is still more time. October 31st is still a few weeks away and there is the possibility of an additional summit before that if we need one'.

Giving evidence to MPs in Westminster, Brexit Secretary Steve Barclay says, 'I can confirm, as the Prime Minister has repeatedly set out, that firstly the government will comply with the law and secondly it will comply with undertakings given to the court in respect of the law'.

Former Brexit Secretary David Davis says he believes a majority of Tory MPs will want to back whatever the Prime Minister brings back from Brussels as it is the 'last play' to secure Brexit, but he also warns against dismissing the Democratic Unionist Party's complaints. 'There will be, quote, a lot of Tory MPs who will take their line from what the DUP do', he tells BBC Radio 4. Reminded that a customs divide in the Irish Sea was once described by DUP leader Arlene Foster as a 'blood red' line, Mr Davis says, 'well let's see when she sees the detail of the deal whether she thinks this is a blood red line or an acceptable compromise'.

Even if there is an agreement before the summit meeting tomorrow, former Justice Secretary David Gauke says pro-Remain MPs would insist on another delay to Brexit to ensure any deal gets full parliamentary scrutiny. Mr Gauke, one of 21 rebels expelled from the Conservative Party, says he and his colleagues would only back a deal if Boris Johnson agrees to ask for more time. 'If he gets a deal I would be supportive', he says, 'but I wouldn't want to be in a position where we vote for a deal on Saturday, something then goes wrong in the next 12 days and we crash out without a deal on October 31st.'

Late in the evening, Michel Barnier, the EU's chief negotiator, tells ambassadors that an agreement has basically been reached, with the possibility of a formal sign-off tomorrow. The Government table a motion for both Houses of Parliament to sit from 9.30am until 2pm on Saturday, which will be voted on by MPs tomorrow. Should the motion pass, the Commons will sit on a Saturday for the first time since the Falklands War in 1982.

Thursday 17th October 2019

14 days to Brexit

The UK and the EU announce that they have agreed a new Brexit deal, and Boris Johnson says he will ask MPs to vote for it on Saturday. The Prime Minister tweets, 'We've got a great new deal that takes back control — now Parliament should get Brexit done on Saturday so we can move on to other priorities like the cost of living, the NHS, violent crime and our environment'. In response, Jean-Claude Juncker tweets, 'Where there is a will, there is a deal - we have one! It's a fair and balanced agreement for the EU and the UK and it is testament to our commitment to find solutions. I recommend that #EUCO endorses this deal.'

The new deal gives the Northern Ireland Assembly at Stormont a vote to leave the new customs arrangements, whereby Northern Ireland remains under EU customs rules, after four years, a unilateral exit mechanism rather than the much maligned backstop which required the EU to consent to changing the deal. It does, however, require only a simple majority vote in Stormont, thus depriving every party there of their current veto. The new deal also introduces customs checks on goods travelling from Great Britain to Northern Ireland if their final destination is the south. Goods bound for Northern Ireland will be charged EU customs duties as they cross the Irish Sea, with the UK Government collecting duties on behalf of the EU. Businesses would then need to reclaim any duties paid on goods consumed wholly in the North. In a joint press conference ahead of the EU summit in Brussels, Boris Johnson says, 'I do think this deal represents a very good deal for the EU and the UK', whilst Jean-Claude Juncker says, 'this is a fair, a balanced agreement. It is testament to our commitment to finding solutions'. Asked if he believes Parliament will approve the deal, the EU President says, 'I hope it will, I'm convinced it will. It has to. Anyway, there will be no prolongation. We have concluded a deal and so there is not an argument for further delay - it has to be done now'.

The DUP's Arlene Foster and Nigel Dodds issue a statement saying that they cannot support the deal, saying, 'We have been involved in ongoing discussions with the Government. As things stand, we could not support what is being suggested on customs and consent issues, and there is a lack of clarity on VAT. We will continue to work with the Government to try and get a sensible deal that works for Northern Ireland and protects the economic and constitutional integrity of the United Kingdom'.

Jeremy Corbyn also dismisses the new deal, issuing a statement saying, 'from what we know, it seems the Prime Minister has negotiated an even worse deal than Theresa May's, which was overwhelmingly rejected. These proposals risk triggering a race to the bottom on rights and protections: putting food safety at risk, cutting environmental standards and workers' rights, and opening up our NHS to a takeover by US private corporations. This sell out deal won't bring the country together and should be rejected. The best way to get Brexit sorted is to give the people the final say in a public vote'. Liberal Democrat leader Jo Swinson echoes his words, saying, 'the fight to stop Brexit is far from over. Boris Johnson's deal would be bad for our economy, bad for our public services, and bad for our environment. The next few days will set the direction of our country for generations, and I am more determined than ever to stop Brexit. When this deal comes to Parliament, we will use every possible opportunity to give the public a People's Vote on the Brexit deal that includes the option to remain in the European Union'.

Nigel Farage, leader of the Brexit Party, says, 'I would much rather we had an extension and a chance of a General Election than accept this dreadful new EU treaty'. He goes on to tell BBC News, 'I would very much like us to leave on October 31st but I understand that the Benn Act has been passed and that makes it impossible', adding, 'if withdrawal agreement four fails on Saturday, as I believe it will, I think then Boris Johnson as Prime Minister would drop the idea of this new treaty and there is a possibility of putting together a Leave alliance for the next General Election'.

In the House of Commons, Sir Oliver Letwin leads attempts to change the timetable for Saturday's sitting during which the new Brexit deal will be debated and voted upon. His motion passes by 287 votes to 275 and means an amendment can be made to the Prime Minister's Bill which withholds Parliamentary consent to the deal until the terms of the Benn Act have been met and the Prime Minister has sent a letter to the EU requesting an extension to Article 50. The former Tory backbencher tells MPs that his motion 'will enable those of us, like me, who wish to support and carry through and eventually see the ratification of this deal, not to put us in the position of allowing the Government off the Benn Act hook on Saturday'.

The DUP reaffirm their stance on the new Brexit deal, with Sammy Wilson telling BBC Radio 4's 'Today' programme, 'I can give you absolute assurance we will not be voting for this deal when it comes before the Commons tomorrow'. Foreign Secretary Dominic Raab says that the Government had 'certainly not given up' on their DUP 'friends' but the responsibility was on 'setting up the deal and to argue for its benefits and its merits in relation to Northern Ireland'. The Thatcherite Bruges Group, which includes Norman Tebbit and Lord Lamont, reveal this morning that it too opposes the Prime Minister's deal, issuing a statement saying, 'we urge members of Parliament who wish to honour the result of the referendum to reject this defective agreement if it is put before them'.

A legal challenge is launched arguing that the proposed deal negotiated with the EU breaches UK law by leaving Northern Ireland in a separate customs arrangement to the rest of the country. The petition is being heard in the Court of Session in Edinburgh, Scotland's highest civil court, which previously ruled Boris Johnson's prorogation of Parliament unlawful. Aidan O'Neill QC, acting for the petitioners, tells the court that the proposed Brexit deal would mean a 'continuing regime of EU law applicable to Northern Ireland', which is contrary to Section 55 of the Taxation (Cross-Border Trade) Act 2018, adding that this would breach the Act's terms by creating different customs rules in Northern Ireland to the rest of the UK, leaving the deal void and unsuitable to be put before Parliament. Mr O'Neill goes on to tell the court, 'what we have before us is a void agreement that has been presented publicly and to Parliament as valid. The agreement which was presented yesterday is void; is of no effect as a matter of law'. The case is later dismissed by the Court, the ruling declaring that, 'the petitioner's applications for interim orders are misconceived and unjustified. They have no or at best a weak prima facie case'.

French President Emmanuel Macron says at the EU summit, 'I think the October 31st date should be respected. I don't think that new deadlines should be given. We need to end these negotiations and get on negotiating the future relationship'. His comments are echoed by Leo Varadkar who says of an extension to Article 50, 'bear in mind that request would have to be agreed unanimously by all 27 leaders, so I don't think MPs voting tomorrow should make the assumption there would be unanimity for an extension'. The Irish Prime Minister goes on to add, 'but our point of view has always been that we would be open to it, but it would be a mistake to assume that it's a guarantee, given that it requires unanimity by all 27 member states'.

On the eve of what has been dubbed as 'Super Saturday' in Parliament, Boris Johnson attempts to woo politicians from different parties with his appeal to 'get Brexit done'. Speaking on ITV about tomorrow's vote he says, 'I think that getting it done would be a chance for us to come together as a country and move on and focus on things that really matter to people. I think the sigh of relief that would go up, not just around Britain, but around the world, would be very, very large and passionate'.

'Super Saturday' in the House of Commons begins at 9.30am with the Speaker announcing that he will allow Sir Oliver Letwin's amendment, and that it will be debated alongside the Prime Minister's motion to approve his deal. In response, the Government let it be known that if MPs approve Sir Oliver's amendment they will pull their own motion, resulting in no 'meaningful' vote on the proposal today. During the ensuing debate, the Prime Minister tells the Commons that the Brexit issue must not be allowed to 'consume' Westminster any more, saying, 'the House will need no reminding that this is the second deal and the fourth vote, three-and-a-half years after the nation voted for Brexit. And during those years, friendships have been strained, families divided and the attention of this House consumed by a single issue that has at times felt incapable of resolution. But I hope that this is the moment when we can finally achieve that resolution and reconcile the instincts that compete within us.'

Sir Oliver's amendment that activates the Benn Act is backed by opposition MPs and ten former Tory rebels, including ex-Chancellor Philip Hammond and former Justice Secretary David Gauke. It is also supported by the DUP, the Prime Minister's last-ditch meetings with the Unionists failing to change their minds and, as a consequence, the amendment passes by 322 votes to 306. After the vote, the Prime Minister confirms that he is pulling his own motion, going on to say, 'I will not negotiate a delay with the EU and neither does the law compel me to', adding that he still intends to bring the legislation for his deal forward and call a new Commons vote on the proposal. After hearing his words SNP MP Joanna Cherry, who was one of the petitioners in the legal case over prorogation, tells the Commons, 'we're back in court on Monday morning and it will be possible then to secure the court's assistance if the Prime Minister has flouted the law and the promises he gave to the court'.

As MPs debated, hundreds of thousands of people gather in Central London to demonstrate in favour of a 'final say' referendum. The Mayor of London, Sadiq Khan, says, 'we are united in believing every form of Brexit is worse than remaining in the European Union', adding, 'Brexit has been a complete and utter mess'. Speaking to jubilant crowds after MPs vote to delay approval for the Prime Minister's deal, shadow Chancellor John McDonnell says, 'we cannot support this deal. It is now time to revert to the fundamental principle that underlies our democracy. Let our people decide. Let democracy reign once again'. Shadow Home Secretary Diane Abbott tells the crowd, 'I am here to support this rally for a People's Vote. I am a Remainer, my constituency is a solid Remain constituency. I have come from defeating Boris and his terrible deal'. Later, footage posted on social media shows Jacob Rees-Mogg, his young son Peter, and Cabinet Minister Andrea Leadsom being heckled by demonstrators as they leave Parliament under police escort to shouts of 'scum' and 'traitor'.

Late in the evening, three letters are sent from the Government to Donald Tusk, the President of the European Council. The first is the letter demanded by the Benn Act, using the exact wording specified in the legislation, which asks the EU to delay Brexit beyond the October 31st deadline. The letter is from the Prime Minister, but is not signed. The second is a covering letter from Sir Tim Barrow, the

UK's Permanent Representative in Brussels, making it clear that the request in the first letter was from Parliament, not the Government. In the third letter, which was signed by Boris Johnson, and was also sent to the leaders of the 27 other EU nations, the Prime Minister distances himself from the first letter, making it clear that he strongly opposes any delay to Brexit. In it, Boris Johnson describes a delay as 'deeply corrosive' which would 'damage the interests' of both sides, the letter going on to say that the UK would continue to ratify the deal and that the Prime Minister urges Brussels to do the same.

The French President's office signals that he would not support an extension to Article 50, with Emanuel Macron quoted as saying that a delay was 'in nobody's interest'.

Boris Johnson's three letter approach provokes anger amongst Remainers. Jolyon Maugham QC, one of those who brought the successful Supreme Court challenge over the prorogation of Parliament, says, 'the Prime Minister is behaving like a spoilt child who cannot do what he wants and so does gracelessly what he must. But ultimately what matters is whether the EU accepts the request for an extension'. Overnight, John McDonnell tweets, 'Johnson is a Prime Minister who is now treating Parliament and the Courts with contempt. His juvenile refusal to even sign the letter confirms what we always suspected that Johnson with his arrogant sense of entitlement considers he is above the law and above accountability'. He adds, 'Message to Johnson. Nobody, no matter how high, is above the law and has the right to tear up our parliamentary constitution'. Sir Kier Starmer tells BBC's Andrew Marr, 'I am sure there will be court proceedings'. The SNP's Westminster leader Ian Blackford says, 'after being defeated on his extreme Brexit deal, Boris Johnson is now attempting to scheme his way out of due process with childish manoeuvres. This is a Tory leader that is simply unfit for the office he holds. Boris Johnson is not above the law and if he does not fully abide by the Benn Act and secure an extension then we will see him in court'.

Both Sir Kier Starmer and John McDonnell suggest that the Labour Party may back a second referendum when Boris Johnson brings his Brexit legislation back to Parliament next week. In his interview with Andrew Marr, the shadow Brexit Secretary says, 'we need an amendment to say that whatever deal gets through, it should be subject to a referendum where that deal is put to the public and they're asked do you want to leave on these terms or would you rather remain in the EU', adding that, 'when that bill goes down it is inevitable that that amendment will be put down'. Asked if the Labour front bench would back the amendment, Sir Kier replies, 'that is the clear policy'. The shadow Chancellor tells Sky News that an amendment for a second vote would 'almost inevitably come up', adding, 'we've always said, if Boris Johnson is confident about this deal, go back to the people with it'.

When asked on Sky News if he could guarantee that the UK will leave the EU by Halloween, Michael Gove replies, 'we have the means and the ability to do so. I think the mood in the country is clear and the Prime Minister's determination is absolute and I am with him in this, we must leave by October 31st.' Mr Gove goes on to warn that yesterday's parliamentary defeat has increased the risk of no deal, saying, 'we cannot guarantee that the European Council will grant an extension'.

Sir Oliver Letwin tells the BBC, 'I am absolutely behind the Government now as long as they continue with this bill, continue with the deal, I will support it, I will vote for it'. Amber Rudd says that she too will vote for the deal, saying there was a 'fragile but sincere coalition of people who want to support it'.

John Bercow sparks anger in the Commons by refusing the Prime Minister's attempt to trigger a meaningful vote on his Brexit deal. Referring to Saturday's debate, the Speaker says, 'it is clear that the motions are in substance the same', adding, 'the motion will not be debated today as it would be repetitive and disorderly to do so'. In response, the Prime Minister's official spokesman says, 'we are disappointed that the Speaker has yet again denied us the chance to deliver on the will of the British people. We will now go ahead with the introduction of the Withdrawal Agreement Bill today, with a second reading tomorrow'.

Judges at Scotland's highest civil court, who have been asked to rule on whether the Prime Minister complied with the Benn Act, delay making a decision until it becomes clear to as to whether the law has been 'complied with in full'.

The government publish The Withdrawal Agreement Bill, a 110 page document accompanied by a 124 page explanatory note. MPs will vote on the Bill for the first time tomorrow evening, and Government sources claim to be confident that they have enough support for it succeed. That vote will be followed by a programme motion calling for the Bill to be passed by the Commons within 72 hours. If the programme motion is defeated, the Government will lose control of the timetable, meaning there would be little chance of getting the law passed by October 31st. Former Tory chief whip Mark Harper says that anyone voting against the timetable would be trying to derail Brexit, adding, 'they cannot hide in plain sight. They will be frustrating Brexit and this House's ability to deliver on the EU referendum result'. Brexit Secretary Stephen Barclay calls on MPs to 'respect the referendum' by backing the Bill, warning them, 'this is the chance to leave the EU with a deal on October 31st', but Sir Kier Starmer responds by accusing the Prime Minister of 'trying to bounce MPs into signing off a Bill that could cause huge damage to our country'.

German Economy Minister Peter Altmaier, a close ally of Angela Merkel, says that the situation in the UK has left European leaders 'not knowing who actually speaks for this country'. Of an extension to Article 50, Mr Altmaier says that he is 'not ideologically opposed to extending again for a few days or a few weeks if you then certainly get a good solution that excludes a hard Brexit'. He goes on to add, 'if the British are to opt for one of the longer-term options, that is, new elections or a new referendum, then it goes without saying that the European Union should do it, for me anyway'.

In the European Parliament, Nigel Farage claims that the Prime Minister has signed up to a deal that 'reduces the UK to the status of a colony of the EU', adding, 'he is doing it because he does not want an election, he wants to bounce us into this new treaty before we wake up'. Jean-Claude Juncker, who is due to stand down as Commission President at the end of the month, tells the Parliament that it has 'pained me to spend so much of this mandate dealing with Brexit. A waste of time and a waste of energy'. Donald Tusk tells MEP's that the latest agreement is 'based on the deal that we agreed with the previous Government', adding, 'Prime Minister Johnson's acceptance to have customs checks at the points of entry into Northern Ireland will allow us to avoid border checks between Ireland and Northern Ireland, and will ensure the integrity of the Single Market'. Of the Prime Minister's letters sent at the weekend, Mr Tusk says, 'the situation is quite complex', adding, 'I am consulting the leaders on how to react, and will decide in the coming days. It is obvious that the result of these consultations will very much depend on what the British Parliament decides, or doesn't decide. We should be ready for every scenario'. Also addressing MEPs, Michel Barnier claims that it will take years to rebuild ties after Brexit, saying, 'we will have to renegotiate for one year, two years, three years, maybe more in some areas, to rebuild all that will have been pulled apart by the desire of those backing Brexit'.

In the UK Parliament, the Prime Minister, facing two crucial votes later, warns, 'I will in no way allow months more of this', going on to say, 'if Parliament refuses to allow Brexit to happen and instead gets its way and decides to delay everything until January or possibly longer, in no circumstances can the Government continue with this'. The Prime Minister goes on to warn that if he is defeated in either of the votes then, 'with great regret I must say the Bill will have to be pulled and we will have to go forward to a General Election. I will argue at that election let's get Brexit done and the leader of the opposition will make his case to spend 2020 having two referendums: one on Brexit and one on Scotland. The people will decide.'

 At 7pm, the House of Commons votes on whether the Withdrawal Agreement Bill should be approved in principle and sent forward for further scrutiny. The Prime Minister wins the vote, by 329 to 299, making his deal the first to be approved by Parliament, but any sense of jubilation is short lived. Immediately afterwards, MPs vote against the timetable motion, asking them to approve the deal within 72 hours, defeating the Government by 322 votes to 308. Immediately after the second vote, the Prime Minister gets to his feet in the Commons and says, 'I must express my disappointment that the house has again voted for delay rather than a timetable that would have guaranteed that the UK would have been in a position to leave the EU on October 31st with a deal. And we now face further uncertainty and the EU must now make up their minds over how to answer Parliament's request for a delay. I will speak to EU member states about their intentions until they have reached a decision. Until we have reached a decision, I am afraid we will pause this legislation. Let me be clear. Our policy remains that we should not delay, that we should leave the EU on October 31st and that is what I will say to the EU and I will report back to the House'.

Jeremy Corbyn tells the Commons that MPs had 'refused to be bounced into debating a hugely significant piece of legislation in just two days with barely any notice and analysis of the economic impact of this Bill'. He goes on to say to the Prime Minister, 'work with us, all of us, to agree a reasonable timetable, and I suspect this House will vote to debate, scrutinise and, I hope, commend the detail of this Bill. That would be the sensible way forward, and that is the offer I make on behalf of the opposition tonight'.

Father of the House, Kenneth Clarke, echoes the sentiments of the Labour leader, saying, 'I can't quite see the logic of pausing progress on the Bill when the whole House is expecting the next two days to be spent on it', adding, 'it would enable us to see how quickly the House is actually proceeding, what sort of time is being looked for, it may enable then, if people start filibustering, which I hope they won't, for the Government to get a majority for a timetable motion if it came back which was a modest adjustment to the one he had, because I think three or four days more would certainly do it'.

Publication of the divisions list reveals that 17 of the 21 rebel Tory MPs sided with the Government on the first vote, but only nine did so on the second. Nineteen Labour MPs rebelled against their frontbench and voted with the Government to approve the deal in principle, but only 5 of them voted for the timetable motion. The DUP voted unanimously against the Government on both motions, as did the Liberal Democrats and the SNP.

The events in Parliament are met with a quick response from Donald Tusk, who tweets, 'Following PM Boris Johnson's decision to pause the process of ratification of the Withdrawal Agreement, and in order to avoid a no deal Brexit, I will recommend the EU27 accept the UK request for an extension. For this I will propose a written procedure.' Taoiseach Leo Varadkar responds to the votes in the Commons by tweeting, 'It's welcome that the House of Commons voted by a clear majority in favour of legislation needed to enact Withdrawal Agreement. We will now await further developments from London and Brussels about next steps including timetable for the legislation and the need for an extension.' Nigel Farage tweets, 'Do or die is over, we have now moved on to dying in a ditch. We will not be leaving the EU on 31st October.'

Shadow Justice Secretary Richard Burgon, a close ally of Jeremy Corbyn, says that Labour would back a General Election 'as soon as no deal is off the table', adding, 'we are not in the business of leaving the Tories in power, we want them out as soon as possible'. Asked about a second referendum first, a policy favoured by a number of Labour frontbenchers, Mr Burgon replies, 'I think that is fantasy politics to be fair because a public vote cannot occur under the current arithmetic of Parliament'.

Referring to Boris Johnson's deal, David Lidington, Theresa May's de-facto deputy when she was in office, tells the BBC, 'my gut instinct is to give it another go because I think even if you end up with an election then tactically we will be seen to have really pressed the Labour Party, to say, well, if two days is not enough then how many days actually would be sufficient for you?' Mr Lidington goes on to say, of a General Election, 'I think the most probable outcome is you are probably looking at the last week in November or the first couple of weeks in December'.

Asked what length of extension he believes the EU will offer the UK, Brexit Party leader Nigel Farage tells the BBC, 'obviously what they want is a General Election or a second referendum, they want some degree of resolution. So, I would have thought at least until the end of January, perhaps even longer'. On a potential election pact with the Conservatives, Mr Farage says, 'I would work with anybody that wanted to honour the result of the referendum for us to leave the European Union and to leave its institutions and to be an independent country, but right at the moment that looks very unlikely'.

German Foreign Minister Heiko Maas echoes reports of French President Emmanuel Macron's view that any further extension to Article 50 did not have to stretch into the new year. 'We need to know, what will be the reason for this?' Mr Maas tells news channel n-tv, adding, 'if it will be about pushing back the date by two or three weeks to allow lawmakers in London to implement the ratification of the exit bill in a reasonable way, I think this will rather not be a problem'. Mr Mass is later overruled by Angela Merkel's spokesman Steffen Seibert, who tells reporters that the UK's extension request would 'not fail due to Germany'.

Leo Varadkar tells the Irish Parliament that Donald Tusk is recommending that the EU27 'accept an extension until January 31st that could be terminated early if the House of Commons and House of Lords ratifies an agreement'. He goes on to add, 'I agreed to that but that's not yet agreed by the 27 and we may have to have an emergency European Council over the course of the next few days to discuss it if he can't get consensus'.

Speaking on Radio 4's 'Today' programme, shadow Business Secretary Rebecca Long-Bailey is asked if Labour would vote for a General Election if the Prime Minister asks for one after the EU grants an extension. She replies, 'that's our position. But we also want the Prime Minister to look at the compromise that's been offered that a lot of MPs support, and that's the ability to be able to properly scrutinise the Bill'. Tory Party chairman, James Cleverly, tells the same programme, 'we've been calling for a General Election, me personally, the Prime Minister at the despatch box, my friends and colleagues all around the country, for months now. The Labour Party are running scared and I can completely understand why, their Brexit message is confused at best'. Mr Cleverly goes on to say that the Government has had to 'ramp up' its' no deal preparations because 'the EU has not agreed an extension and therefore it is absolutely essential that we make sure that we are ready to leave'.

In the Commons, Nigel Dodds, the DUP's leader in Westminster, tells the Brexit Secretary that Northern Ireland could be plunged into political instability if the Prime Minister's Brexit deal becomes law. He tells Steve Barclay, 'you are really in danger here of causing real problems with the Belfast Agreement, the St Andrews Agreement, the political institutions and the political stability in Northern Ireland by what you are doing to the Unionist community. Please wake up and realise what is happening here. We need to get our heads together and look at a way forward that can solve this problem. Don't plough ahead regardless, I urge you'.

Boris Johnson manages to win the support of MPs for his legislative programme, the Queens Speech being passed in the Commons by 310 votes to 294. The Liberal Democrats had put forward an amendment to the Queen's Speech calling for the Prime Minister's Brexit deal to be put to a national vote against the option to Remain, but Speaker John Bercow decided not to select the amendment.

In a letter to Jeremy Corbyn, the Prime Minister sets out a proposal to resolve the Brexit deadlock, saying, 'if the EU offers the delay that Parliament has requested - that is, we must stay in until 31st January - then it is clear that there must be an election. We cannot risk further paralysis. In these circumstances, the Commons will vote next week on whether to hold an election on December 12th. This would mean that Parliament would dissolve just after midnight on 6th November'. The Prime Minister goes on to tell Mr Corbyn that it was their 'duty to end this nightmare and provide the country with a solution as soon as we reasonably can', adding that if Labour backs his election proposition then the Government 'will make available all possible time between now and 6th November' for key Brexit legislation to be passed. The letter goes on to say that 'Parliament has refused to take decisions' and that it 'cannot refuse to let voters replace it with a new Parliament that can make decisions' before addressing the Labour leader's publicly stated position on a General Election. 'You have repeatedly said that once the EU accepts Parliament's request for a delay until 31st January then you would immediately support an election', the Prime Minister writes before concluding, 'I assume this remains your position and therefore you will support an election next week so the voters can replace this broken Parliament'.

Jeremy Corbyn responds to the Prime Minister in a TV interview this evening by saying, 'take no deal off the table and we absolutely support a general election'. His view is contradicted, however, by Ben Bradshaw, a senior Labour backbencher, who says he is not prepared to back an election. Mr Bradshaw says, 'I think the overwhelming view of Labour MPs and Labour supporters in the country is we need a referendum first before an election'. The SNP, Liberal Democrats and Plaid Cymru also refuse to give their backing to the Prime Minister's plan.

Visiting a hospital in Milton Keynes, Boris Johnson declares that 'nobody will believe that the Labour Party is really going to allow Brexit to happen unless there is a deadline of an election'. The Prime Minister goes on to say, 'as far as I can see, at the moment, the Labour Party is split from top to bottom, and they can't work out whether or not they're in favour of an election, which is the thing they're supposed to be campaigning for the last three-and-a-half years'. He concludes by saying to Jeremy Corbyn, 'man up, let's have an election'. Speaking to Richard and Judy on 'This Morning', Mr Corbyn says, 'I've said all along - take no deal off the table, and we'll have the election', but adds, 'the 12th of December date is really odd for many reasons. It's so near Christmas, it's after universities have ended their terms, etc'.

Michel Barnier holds a meeting with ambassadors in Brussels after which the EU confirms that the bloc has agreed there will be an extension to Article 50, but not how long it will be. The ambassadors will delay their ruling until Monday or Tuesday next week in order to give Jeremy Corbyn more time to decide if he will back a General Election. Sources suggest that President Macron is reluctant to grant an extension to January, his European affairs minister, Amélie de Montchalin, saying, 'we need facts in order to make a decision. We will not deal in political fiction'.

Saturday 26th October 2019

5 days to Brexit

The Brexit process remains in deadlock, with the Labour Party refusing to approve a General Election until the EU grants an extension to Article 50, and the EU reluctant to grant an extension of any significant length until it is sure there will be a General Election. Asked how the impasse could be broken, Jeremy Corbyn replies, 'it depends what the European Union says on Monday or Tuesday about the length of an extension and what the terms of that extension are, so we can't really go any further forward until we have a response from them'.

Business Minister Kwasi Kwarteng tells the BBC, 'I think it will be very difficult to leave on October 31st precisely because of the Benn Act, the surrender act, which essentially gave authority to the EU, the other side, about whether we will leave on October 31st or not. It looks like they may well give us an extension'. Mr Kwarteng says of Jeremy Corbyn's apparent reluctance to allow a General Election, 'it is an odd position that he is in. For two years he has said, nearly every week at PMQs, that we should have an election while Theresa May was Prime Minister. And now he is saying the opposite'.

It emerges that the Liberal Democrats are ready to offer Boris Johnson a way to sidestep the Labour Party and allow him to secure an election before Christmas. They are said to be proposing a one-page bill which would amend the Fixed Term Parliaments Act to state that the next election will take place on 9th December, three days earlier than under the Prime Minister's proposal. The bill would include a clause that states that the new election date would be cancelled should the EU fail to grant a three-month Brexit extension. The SNP signal that they are prepared to back the plan.

A poll conducted by Opinium shows the Conservative Party on 40 percent, a 16 point lead over Labour. The Lib Dems drop 1 point against the same poll 8 days ago, leaving them on 15 percent, with the Brexit Party on 10 percent.

The Prime Minister tells 'The Mail on Sunday', 'my worry is this Parliament will just waste the next three months like it's wasted the last three years. If Parliament cannot agree a way forward, then it is time for a new Parliament – and the only means of doing this is via a General Election', adding that if Labour 'refuse this timetable – if they refuse to go the extra mile to complete Brexit, I will have no choice but to conclude that they are not really sincere in their desire to get Brexit done'.

Culture Secretary Nicky Morgan is dismissive about the Liberal Democrats plan for a 9th December election but refuses to confirm that the Government would vote against it, saying it would have to wait and see what is in the paperwork. She tells Sky's Ridge on Sunday, 'what is different about the offer, or stunt I might say, by the SNP and Lib Dems is they have obviously made it clear that they have no intention of wanting Brexit to be done, no intention of wanting the Withdrawal Bill', adding, 'if the SNP and Lib Dems want an election then they have a chance to vote for one as quickly as tomorrow when the Government's motion is voted on. We will see if they are in our lobby or not'.

The shadow Chancellor attacks the Lib Dems plan too, tweeting, 'Stunt by the Lib Dems & SNP this morning looks like it's come a cropper with Johnson stealing idea for own purposes. The Lib Dems & SNP may have given up on a People's Vote. We haven't. It's the only way to resolve this issue and stand any chance of bringing country back together'. Shadow Health Secretary Jon Ashworth dismisses the Lib Dems proposed bill as an 'opportunistic stunt', telling Sky News, 'I mean it's entirely ridiculous. It would need cross-party support to get through the House of Commons procedures and then it would be subject to all kinds of amendments, particularly when it gets into the House of Lords'. He goes on to add, 'it's just a stunt so the Lib Dems can get on the telly today'.

Former Chancellor Philip Hammond tells Sky News that he will not vote for an early General Election in the Commons tomorrow. He tells Sophie Ridge, 'I will vote against it. This is not the time for a General Election. This is a time for cool heads and grown-up Government,' adding, 'the Government should stop making threats, stop throwing tantrums, and get on with the grown-up business of doing its business. Just because it can't get exactly what it wants doesn't mean it should stop working'.

Labour frontbencher Lucy Powell tells Radio 4's the 'Westminster Hour' that an 'election soon is now both inevitable and necessary'. She goes on to add, 'Parliament is in a deadlock and we need to break that deadlock somehow, even if Brexit is done. The issue is the terms of that election, the when and how of that election. I think what we've seen from the Liberal Democrats and the SNP is trying to shape the terms of that election in a way that would favour them the most, it's pure playing of politics.'

Monday 28th October 2019

3 days to Brexit

Donald Tusk announces an extension to Article 50. In a tweet, the President of the European Council says, 'The EU27 has agreed that it will accept the UK's request for a #Brexit flextension until 31 January 2020. The decision is expected to be formalised through a written procedure.' Under the terms of the extension, the UK will be able to quit the bloc before January 31st if Parliament is able to agree to the Prime Minister's deal. If MPs back the deal in November the UK will leave the EU on December 1st and if they back the deal in December then the UK will leave the EU on January 1st. Michel Barnier, the EU's chief Brexit negotiator, says, 'I'm very happy that a decision has been taken'.

Jo Swinson tells the BBC Radio 4 'Today' programme that there were various reasons why her proposal for an election on December 9th makes more sense than the Prime Minister's plan to go to the polls on 12th December. 'Clearly, it's three further days away from Christmas and I understand that the public appetite for an election around Christmas is not necessarily high so I think, from the point of view of the economy and retailers, keeping it as far away as possible is helpful,' she says. The Lib Dems plan for a single line Bill to bypass the Fixed Term Parliament Act, and thus require only a simple majority in the Commons to trigger a General Election, bypasses the need to have the Labour Party on board and appears to be gaining traction within Government circles. Miss Swinson goes on to say, 'what waiting would do is risk no deal, because if we waste this extension and we end up in January with that 31st of January deadline looming, and we haven't done anything with this time, then there's no guarantee the EU will extend again and then no deal is back on the table'. Shadow Chancellor John McDonnell reacts to Ms Swinson's proposal by tweeting, 'Looks like the Lib Dem and Tory pact of 2010 is being re-established. They are back together, selling out the People's Vote campaign and the cross party campaign to prevent a no deal. The Lib Dems will stop at nothing to get their ministerial cars back.'

In the Commons, the Prime Minister tables another motion under the Fixed Term Parliament Act, this time requesting a General Election on 12th December. Opening up the debate, Boris Johnson says, 'we will not allow this paralysis to continue. This House can no longer keep the country hostage. Millions of families and businesses cannot plan for the future', accusing Jeremy Corbyn of 'running away from the judgment of the British people'. During the debate Labour, the SNP and the Liberal Democrats all indicate that they will not support the motion, with the SNP and the Lib Dems inviting the Prime Minister to support their proposal for an election on December 9th. In response, Independent Group leader Anna Soubry says of the Liberal Democrats, 'they have, in my view, turned their back on the People's Vote, wrongly claiming there is no majority for it in Parliament. I am sorry to say that old style, selfish, tribal party politics is at play'. Predictably, the motion fails, the Government securing only 299 of the 434 votes needed for the super majority required to trigger a General Election. Speaking immediately after the vote, the Prime Minister tells the Commons that he will introduce a one line bill tomorrow, similar to the one proposed by the Lib Dems and the SNP, to set aside the Fixed Term Parliament Act and enable an election on 12th December.

During the debate in the Commons, the Prime Minister's letter to Donald Tusk, accepting the EU's extension, is released. In it, Boris Johnson complains that he has no 'discretion' to refuse the 'unwanted' postponement, and urges European leaders to rule out pushing the deadline back any further. His letter goes on to say, 'while we will of course not seek to deliberately disrupt the EU's business, I must underline that I continue to have a responsibility as Prime Minister to protect the UK's national interests during this period, including in EU decision-making. I would have much preferred it if the UK Parliament could have proceeded rapidly to ratify the deal we reached between us. Unfortunately, I very much fear that this Parliament will never do so as long as it has the option of further delay'. Later in the evening, Whitehall announces the suspension of 'Operation Yellowhammer', signalling the halting of the Government's preparations for no deal.

Contradicting his party leader, Angus MacNeil, a senior SNP MP, warns against handing the Prime Minister the 'Christmas present' of a December election. He says, 'we would be better having a referendum than an election, which can gift one side victory with 35 per cent of the vote', saying of the Prime Minister, 'we have currently got him in a cage'. Former Cabinet minister David Gauke, one of 21 Tory MPs suspended for opposing no deal, also cautions against a December poll, saying 'when someone opens the front door to a stranger in December, they expect to be sung a carol, not asked how they are going to vote'.

Jeremy Corbyn changes his mind about a December General Election saying, 'we have now heard from the EU that the extension of Article 50 to 31st January has been confirmed, so for the next three months, our condition of taking no deal off the table has now been met. We will now launch the most ambitious and radical campaign for real change our country has ever seen'. Announcing his decision at Labour's London HQ, Mr Corbyn says, 'there will be a parliamentary process this afternoon. We are going out there to fight an election campaign and I can't wait to get out there on the streets.'

After Mr Corbyn's announcement, Labour campaign group Momentum tweet, 'Labour are officially backing an election. This is the opportunity of a lifetime to put an end to the shambolic mess the Tories have made and return hope to millions. Let's do this.' Shadow Justice Secretary Richard Burgon tells Sky News that Labour will campaign on a 'manifesto of hope'. 'We are up for the fight and we believe we are going to win it,' he says.

Labour backbencher Neil Coyle criticises the decision, saying, 'today could be crucial. We have limited chances to get a People's Vote but anyone backing an election will prevent it, as well as allowing Johnson to bring back no deal. I know where I stand and am disgusted at those putting party politics before the national interest'. His view is echoed by Barry Sheerman, Labour MP for Huddersfield, who tweets, 'A clear majority of our Shadow Cabinet were against a December election yesterday but Jeremy Corbyn has been persuaded to override them after interventions from Milne and Karie Murphy'. Mr Sheerman goes on to tell Sky News that it was 'sheer madness to hold the General Election in December and on Boris Johnson's agenda'.

The Prime Minister opens the debate on his one line bill proposing a General Election on 12th December by saying that time had come to 'refresh the Parliament and have the people decide'. Gesturing across the Commons, he says, 'all they want to do is procrastinate', adding, 'they don't want to deliver Brexit on October 31st, on November 31st, even on January 31st.They just want to spin it out forever, until the 12th of never. And when the 12th of never eventually comes around, they'll devise one of their complicated parliamentary procedures and move a motion for a further delay and a further extension then'. During his response to the Prime Minister's address, in which he declares Labour ready and willing to fight a General Election, Jeremy Corbyn is challenged by Paul Farrelly, the Labour MP for Newcastle-under-Lyme. Mr Farrelly tells his party leader, 'I will be voting against an early election today and encourage as many of my colleagues as possible to defy the threats and blandishments to do so. The reality is that the uncertainty of a General Election most certainly does not take no deal off the table'.

As the debate went on in the chamber, Boris Johnson restores the Tory whip to 10 of the 21 Conservative rebels who were expelled after backing the Benn Act. The Prime Minister meets with the 10 MPs in his House of Commons office to offer them the chance to return to the Tory fold. All 10 accept the offer, and will now be able to stand as Tory candidates at the forthcoming General Election. The 10 who have had the Tory whip restored are: Alistair Burt, Caroline Nokes, Greg Clark, Sir Nicholas Soames, Ed Vaizey, Margot James, Richard Benyon, Stephen Hammond, Steve Brine and Richard Harrington. The remaining 11 rebels, including Philip Hammond and Ken Clarke, are not made a similar offer.

Later in the afternoon, Jeremy Corbyn tables an amendment to the Bill which would allow 16 and 17-year-olds and EU nationals to vote, but the Deputy Speaker, Sir Lindsay Hoyle, selects only one amendment; to change the date of the election to 9th December. That amendment is defeated by 315 votes to 295 and then the Bill itself is passed by 438 votes to 20, confirming that the UK will face its first December General Election in almost a century, the country still none the wiser as to when, or even if, the Brexit hell will ever end.

THE END

FOR NOW

....

www.ingramcontent.com/pod-product-compliance
Lightning Source LLC
Chambersburg PA
CBHW031239250726
48655CB00005B/2016